INTEREST RATE ANALYTICS

Dedicated to my colleagues

TABLE OF CONTENTS

INTRODUCTION

A better understanding of interest rates can give investors, creditors and even policymakers insight into the world of business, investing and economics. It is also hoped that this study of interest rates can help lay a groundwork for future economic prosperity.

Interest Rate Analytics is divided into five parts which include the appendices: Part I presents a classification of interest rates into six basic types. Part II surveys over two centuries of thought on interest rates beginning with Adam Smith (1776). Part III explores a derivation of interest rates that incorporates the borrower's debt service coverage and full loan payoff. The brief Part IV compares the returns on various types of debt that carry the same *apparent* interest rate. The appendices also provide extensive supporting information, additional economic and financial commentary as well as a suggested blueprint for future economic expansion.

The core of *Interest Rate Analytics* is the concept of *credit-based interest rates* discussed in Part III of this book. Credit-based interest rates are believed to be an instructive tool because the interest rates computed embody the information about the financial strength and debt service capacity of economic entities (with a focus on businesses here), with the essential assumption that the debts are paid *in full*. Moreover, the computations are based on observable phenomena and Generally Accepted Accounting Principles (GAAP). Comparing credit-based interest rates by firms and sectors also can also help gauge prevailing economic conditions as well as to identify the emergence of any significant deviations from policy interest rates.

The book is a draft overview with shortcomings that further study and collaborative work can improve upon. It is hoped that the essentials are presented without too many errors, omissions, misinterpretations, or oversimplifications. The reader is encouraged to consult other resources to supplement an understanding of the topics.

PART I

INTEREST RATE CLASSIFICATION

Interest can be briefly defined as a price paid by someone (a borrower) for using someone else's (the lender's) resources for a certain period of time, with the assumption that those resources will be returned in full to the lender. This price is usually expressed as a percentage (for example 6%) of the amount borrowed (the principal balance of the loan). The resources can include cash/money or goods/inventory on credit.

Interest rates are classified in five basic categories here. The sixth category, *credit-based interest rates,* is a core topic of the book further elaborated upon in Part III.

1. Stated Interest Rate
2. Loan Rate, Yield and Pricing (banking context)
3. Yield (debt markets/bond context)
4. Policy Interest Rates (official rates)
5. The real interest rate (equilibrium, natural).
6. Credit-based interest rate

1. Stated Interest Rate

The first category of interest rate is that which is stated on the loan document as a percentage of the amount lent. For example, a stated rate of 6% on a $100 loan should in the simplest sense mean that the interest amount due should be equal to $6 per year (the actual amount of interest paid each year may vary from this for reasons to be covered elsewhere; for a 6% loan that matures in less than one year, then the 6% is an *annualized* figure). For bonds, the stated rate may also be called the "coupon", and the "note rate" for a (bank) loan. For vendor financing in a business context (accounts/notes receivable and trade payables), there may be a stated rate in the terms of financing; such loans would be expected to be short-term.

2. Loan Rate, Pricing and Yield (banking context)

When businesses or individuals borrow from a bank, their debt to the bank is a typically called a bank loan, although there are many types, including business loans, real estate loans (such as home loans and commercial real estate loans) and personal loans. Some bank loans may be sold off, or remain as part of the bank loan portfolio. Loans that remain on a bank portfolio may not have a market value assigned to them or may not be marked-to-market.

The interest rate on bank loans is based on a process of *loan pricing* in order to calculate a yield that is specific to banking that is intended to give the bank adequate profitability. The profitability of a loan to the bank is essentially computed by subtracting the bank's expenses associated with the loan from the income expected from the loan.

Sources of funds for banks. When banks borrow funds to lend out to their customers, there is a cost to the bank for using those funds; not surprisingly, this is often called the "cost of funds" (COF). The COF may also be called the *matched maturity funding rate*; "matched maturity" means that the funds that the bank borrows match the maturity (term) of the loan.

Gross Interest Margin (also may be called Net Loan Revenue) is equal to the *loan interest rate* minus the bank's cost of funds.
Example. A bank borrows funds to lend out to a customer. Assume that the bank's cost of funds is 3.5%. If the loan rate that the bank offers the borrowing customer is 7%, the gross interest margin is 7% - 3.5% =3.5%. If bank policy guidelines indicate a target loan yield range of 3.5% this loan is within the target profitability guidelines.

Other Income. The bank has other potential sources of income including *deposit income*, the method by which the interest is collected (some *interest collection methods* are more profitable), and *loan fees*. Because some loans are made to borrowers that have many other loans and banking relationships including at the branch, a wide variety of sources of income may be included to gain a picture of the profitability of the overall relationship with the customer. Therefore, while an individual loan might therefore not be particularly profitable, when the entire relationship with the customer is taken into account the bank may still be within its target profitability range.

Other costs to the bank include costs of servicing (managing) the loan, and an estimate for the cost of provision for loan losses and non-accruals ("bad" loans). Banks estimate the costs of bad loans according to a method of loan grading which can vary across banks. In business lending, the strongest borrowers might have a loan grade of 3, with most borrowers in the 4 to 5 range. So-called "problem credits" might be in the 6 to 9 range, depending on the bank's policy and loan grade scale.

Pricing Base

London Interbank Offered Rate (LIBOR). LIBOR is a floating rate quoted by the individual banks contained in the Libor panel (Michaud and Upper, 2008). Swap rates serve as a pricing base for Libor-based loans (floating rates can be swapped into fixed rates in the swap market). For example, for a term loan with a 5-year maturity funded with 1-month LIBOR, the pricing base rate in this case would be the 5-yr swap rate (matched maturity at 5 years) at say 5% while the cost of funds (1-month LIBOR) might be 3.5%. The customer would be quoted a spread over this base rate as *Swap +2%* and customer's interest rate would be 5%+2%=7%.

Note that if a customer were to be offered a variable-rate loan priced *specifically* at LIBOR + 2.5%, then the pricing base rate (LIBOR) would be the *same* as the cost of funds to the bank (LIBOR), and the spread between the loan interest rate and the COF would be 2.5%.

Prime Rate. A traditional pricing base for variable-rate loans is the "Prime rate." The Prime rate is not the cost of funds for a bank; it is a *pricing base rate* that banks typically use for quoting commercial loans. It is a pricing "base" because the customer is quoted an interest rate in terms of this base: For example, *Prime + 1*. A customer who receives bank financing *at* the prime rate (Prime + 0) is generally considered to be financially strong and a valued customer of the bank ("prime" in the sense of "preferred" rate). The interest rate for other borrowing customers might be somewhat above the prime rate, such as Prime+1-1/2, Prime + 2 and so on. Bank policy may determine the "spread" (a margin of profit) between the bank's cost of funds and Prime. For example, if the customer interest rate is P+1 and the bank policy spread is 1.25%, then the spread between the customer rate and the cost of funds would be 2.25%.

Other traditional pricing bases include Certificate of Deposit (CD) rates, or for agricultural loans, a Base Agricultural Rate (BAR).

3. Yield (debt markets/ bond context)

Background. The term yield arises primarily for debt (debt instruments) that are traded (i.e. bought and sold) on a (debt) market. Debt that trades on a market can be called a *marketable* debt security. The value of the debt is established on the market (market value or price).

Broadly speaking, the borrowers whose debt may be marketable are private entities (firms/businesses) or public entities (public meaning government entities from the national to the local government level. Municipal bonds are an example of the debt of municipalities (cities). Debts of individuals, including student loans and credit card loans, can also be "packaged" and may trade on debt markets as well.

The type of debt most commonly referred to here will simply be a generic *bond*. Investments in debt such as bonds can be referred to as *fixed income investments*.

5

Yield and Total Return.

Perhaps a way to more easily understand debt (bonds) is to see them from the perspective of how an investor can make money from investing in debt. Investors in debt instruments can be individuals, businesses, banks, bond funds and other entities and can be broadly referred to as *bondholders*.

Total return is the money-making part. The expectation of a positive *total return* on bonds generally helps induce investors to invest in bonds. *Total return* is fundamentally linked to the concept of yield.

The yield itself is a kind of "moving" interest rate that results from the changing *price/value* of a marketable debt security in debt markets. The yield tends to move *inversely* with the price of the bond (i.e. going in the opposite direction).

The *total* return of a bond can be classified into two types of return: *Interest income*, and *capital appreciation*. Periodic payments of interest are made to the bondholder. Capital appreciation results from an increase in the *market price* of the bond. The return from capital appreciation is viewed as fundamentally distinct from the return from *interest income*. Return from capital appreciation requires that in order to realize cash, the investor must either liquidate, or borrow against, the appreciated debt instrument.

There are also investment vehicles such as *fixed income funds* or *bond funds* that aim for income both in the form of interest income and capital appreciation of debt securities.

The yield cannot be discussed without consideration of *policy interest rates* since bond yields can be influence by policy interest rates in our modern monetary system. Policy interest rates will be discussed in the next section below.

Total return Example #1: Declining Interest Rate Environment. As stated above, the yield can be thought of as a "moving" interest rate that is adjusted by the price of the bond (in opposite directions). We begin with a bond investor **Investor A,** who purchases a "plain vanilla" bond with a 6% *coupon* (stated interest rate). For a 6% coupon bond bought at exactly par of $1000 with a semi-annual payments, Investor A receives $30 interest twice a year ($30 x 2) for a total of $60 of interest income per year. Initially the yield of this bond should be 6% ($60/.06=$1000). Assume that the market yields are in the 6% range for now.

Now, assume that overall debt market interest rates decline to 5%. The reason for this decline are not elaborated upon here, but may often be the result of *policy interest rates,* to be discussed in the next section.

Investor B. An investor new to the market who is thinking of investing in a bond now faces a 5% market (5% yield on debt securities). The previous 6% yields are no longer available in the debt marketplace. If **Investor B** wants a bond, the yield is 5%.

Back to **Investor A**: Recall that the coupon (stated rate) of 6% ($60) continues to be paid on the bond until maturity. Given this new bond yield environment of 5% (down from 6%) the price of this bond adjusts upwards. $60 of interest income per year is 5% of a *new* bond price as follows: $60/.05=$1,200. At 5% yields, **Investor B** would be paying $1,200 for the bond. For lucky **Investor A**, who was holding the bond when this change of interest rates occurred, the extra $200 ($1,200 of new value minus the original $1,000 purchase price) represents *capital appreciation.* Say **Investor A** sells the bond to **Investor B**. Investor realizes a profit (also called "capital gain") of $200 and **Investor B** now receives interest income of $60 a year representing a 5% yield ($60/$1200).

The above example was for a falling interest rate environment. It is important to note that in a *rising interest rate environment*, the

opposite situation could be expected to occur, where **Investor A** would suffer a capital loss.

Total Return Example #2: Credit Risk. Briefly, a high-yield (or "junk") bond is a bond whose issuer is evaluated as representing a higher credit risk (risk of default) on its borrowings. The following example illustrates an example of a *capital loss* rather than a capital gain.

Using the same information from above, **Investor A** decides to purchase a 6% coupon bond issued by a company that has a fairly good credit rating (e.g. Moody's, Standard & Poors, etc.). A few years later the company begins to suffer from financial problems. **Investor A** is still receiving interest income of $60 per year. However, the market value (price) of the bond declines to say 500 because of concerns that the company might default on its debt and maybe go bankrupt. At this point the bond becomes "high yield" to new investors. Unfortunately, **Investor A** has now suffered an (unrealized) *capital loss* (the loss is "realized" when sold). Say **Investor B**, seeking a high yield on investment, buys the bond at the new (lower) market price of $500 from **Investor A**. **Investor B** receives the $60 of interest income per year, but since only $500 was paid for the bond, the yield that **Investor B** earns is much higher than 6%, as follows: 60/500=0.12 or 12% per year. While this may be an attractive yield, keep in mind that if the company continues to deteriorate and no longer can make the interest payments (and/or repay the original principal), **Investor B** also could suffer a capital loss.

Government Debt. It should be noted that the bonds of government entities that have financial problems of their own can also result in capital losses for investors. However, for national governments it can be argued that because of their access to central bank financing the risk of default may be lower in the sense that the debt will be repaid by money creation, if necessary. However, *default by inflation* is a theoretical possibility, in which the government bond is repaid in full with interest but the value of the currency has been debased to the point that the money received is virtually worthless (i.e. the purchasing power of the currency has declined to near zero). Although this case is extreme and rare in history (usually due to wrenching political events including war and/or severe long-term mismanagement), it does raise the point that over time a decline in purchasing power can affect the yield to compensate for the loss due to inflation. For a discussion on improved economic management at the national level, see the Appendix.

Other Factors Influencing Yield. The yield cannot be discussed without consideration of *policy interest rates* and *inflation* rates. Policy interest rates will be discussed in the section below, and inflation elsewhere in this study.

Yields on Other Investments. Changes in the yield on bonds and other debt market investments, particularly if policy interest rates are the driving force, are not limited to the debt markets. The prices and yields of other income-producing assets/investments in the economy, including real estate and stocks (equities), can be affected (and possibly as well as the prices of assets that do not produce income).

Non-Marketable Debt. Many types of debt (loans) are not traded on a market, including some bank loans and government debt.

4. Policy Interest Rates (official rates).

Policy interest rates can be a significant force in securities markets (for both debt and equity) and in other asset markets (i.e. real estate). While *policy interest rates* can significantly affect markets they are considered to be essentially generated *externally* from the market.

Types. Policy interest rates can impact other interest rates (including bank loan rates discussed below) as well as the yield and prices of debt securities such as bonds (and other investments). An example of an important policy interest rate is the Federal Fund Rate of the Federal Reserve Bank of the United States. For banks, the London Interbank Offered Rate (LIBOR) might be considered a policy interest rate, but not necessarily an independent one --it is possible that changes in LIBOR rates do not stray too far from the interest rate policies of central banks.

Objectives and priorities. In short, the policy interest rate is used as a tool to influence the economy through monetary policy and to provide financing for various entities, as well as a broad source of financing (liquidity) to the markets.

There are a number of possible reasons for decisions to change policy interest rates. For example, an economy in recession might lead monetary authorities decide on lowering the policy interest rate(s). Conversely, an inflationary economy might lead to a decision to raise interest rates.

For example, policy interest rates may be lowered to give relief to over-indebted borrowers including government entities (which can be major borrowers in debt markets), or to induce new borrowings to stimulate economic activity, and to give bondholders capital appreciation and higher total returns (noted above) as a reward for holding bonds; the capital gains can also provide a form of economic stimulus as the proceeds from these gains can be used to invest elsewhere including the stock and real estate markets.

Inflation (roughly defined as increases in prices) and *inflation expectations* can affect the market value and yields of bonds, and are of concern to monetary authorities. Rising inflation constitutes a decline in purchasing power, making bonds less attractive to invest in without a rise in yields and decline in market prices of the bonds. The topic of inflation in the calculation of the *modern* version of the real interest rate will be discussed in the historical section (the Fisher equation) and in the Appendix regarding *currency dilution*.

Policy interest rates and capital accumulation. Piketty (2014) raises the concern of disproportionate growth in returns to capital, although his analysis is not necessarily in the context of policy interest rates. A by-product of policy interest rates is the potential for an outsized accumulation of wealth based on non-market factors, particularly in an international context: The capital appreciation of debt instruments (discussed above in the yield section), the carry trade and currency appreciation. In the carry trade, investors can take advantage of policy-controlled interest rate differentials across borders. For example, if interest rates are held lower in Japan than in the U.S., income can be earned by borrowing in Japanese yen and investing the borrowed funds in higher-interest paying bonds in the U.S. Moreover, to the extent that higher interest rates in the U.S. leads to appreciation in the U.S. dollar relative to the Yen, the value of assets denominated in that appreciated currency (the U.S. dollar) also rises, giving investors a capital gain in their home currency (Yen in this example).

Information asymmetry and persistent accumulation. A finer point is that although much of the increase in income and wealth inequality may be attributable to capital gains, such income can be highly *volatile*, with losses likely to offset gains, at least in part. The particular concern here is an abnormally *persistent* wealth accumulation (persistence of gains without corresponding losses); in such cases, *information asymmetry* should be considered. Policy interest rates are a particularly valuable source of information because persistent *advance knowledge* of decisions regarding policy interest rates (as well as official exchange rates, bond market interventions and tapers) can translate into a remarkable edge to accumulate wealth for those who may be given selective access to this information. (Note that gains can also occur with well-timed shorts in down markets in the event of a tapering, for example).

Briefly, it should be added that a distinction should be drawn between (a) wealth being amassed from the policy-based/ non-market sources discussed above and (b) fortunes based predominantly on the building of businesses in a largely market-based context. It is however recognized that even in capitalist-oriented economies and competitive market systems the complete

11

absence of policy distortions and special advantages to businesses may be unlikely (Stockman, 2013)

5. The real interest rate (equilibrium, natural)

The *real interest rate* (alternatively referred to as the *equilibrium* or *natural* rate of interest or NRI) appears to have at least two definitions. The earlier (18th-19th century) classical definition appears to have been largely replaced by a modern 20th century version. Briefly stated, the classical real interest rate was originally an interest rate related to measures of profitability or expected profitability on capital investment for firms. The version described by Adam Smith clarified the link between profits and interests, with movements in rates according to the rate of profit.

An important point is the "gap" between official (or policy) rates of the banking system and the equilibrium interest rate (Wicksell 1898, Ropke 1936). Ropke refers to "…the widening of the gap between the rate of interest and profits on capital."(1936:114). If policy/bank rates do not adjust with the equilibrium interest rate, excessive credit expansion or contraction may ensue.

In the 20th century, the Fisher equation, to be discussed further in the historical section, appears to have replaced this earlier definition, and defines the real interest rate as the *nominal* interest rate minus the rate of *inflation* (inflation being defined in various ways to be discussed elsewhere; also see the comments on *currency dilution* in the Appendix). In 20th and 21st century economics, the Fisherian version of the interest rate is generally estimated with the aid of macro-econometric models.

In both cases, the real interest rate is expected to approximately fit into the other categories of interest rates discussed here (stated rate, loan rate, yields) *with the exception of policy interest rates* which are assumed to originate externally-by committee decision.

In the 21st century there has been a revived interest among policymakers to compare the gap between policy interest rates and the estimated real interest rate (Laubach and Williams 2003, Lundvall and Westermark 2011, Manrique and Marques 2004).

The historical section provides more detail on both versions of this type of interest rate.

6. Credit-based Interest Rate:

The *credit-based interest rate* is elaborated upon in Part III and is defined as the interest rate based on the evaluation of the borrower's creditworthiness and full amortization of the principal balance of the loan. The methodology for computing the interest rate fundamentally differs from the loan rate computation in the banking context. Lending institutions typically arrive at the interest rate based on their cost of funds plus a *spread*; a factor for credit risk based is then incorporated as an additional cost which may raise the interest rate. The credit-based interest rate computes the interest rate directly according to the capacity of the firm to service its debt; the debt service coverage (DSC) ratio is the primary measure to determine this capacity.

The interest rate computed can be positive, zero or negative. In the case of a negative interest rate the borrower cannot service the debt at the specified debt service coverage ratio and is likely to be over-indebted; a restructuring of the debt may be necessary.

Although the focus of this research is business lending, a credit-based approach could be applied to other borrowing entities. An advantage of the credit-based approach is that the interest rate is computed based on financial data that is observable. The problem of estimation of macro-economic variables based on "unobservable" data is avoided.

The credit-based approach suggests that there no single interest rate; rather, there are as many interest rates as there are economic entities. The question might arise as to why banks don't use a credit-based approach to computing interest rates.

First, there appears to be no uniformly agreed-upon measure of a primary source of repayment (SOR) from businesses. Various definitions are discussed in the appendix, with the most common one for banks being *(net) cash flow from operations*, which as clarified later is not considered to be a best approximation of the primary SOR.

Second, even if the SOR were agreed upon, the approach of computing a loan rate for a customer based on their SOR and a debt service coverage ratio does not fit into the traditional framework of computing a *COF + spread* as explained in the section on Loan Rates above. The question would arise "where's the spread?"

The "spread" contained in credit-based interest rates is not apparent until market forces (demand and supply factors) are taken into account. In a market, firms that can support a higher interest rate would be those that would in theory be more attractive (profitable) borrowers for a lender, their "bid" would win; the process of capital allocation would then continue to the next highest bidder and so on. However, in the current monetary system, credit rationing is less likely to be an issue because of plentiful supply of credit through credit creation – the ability of the monetary system to create credit upon a base of excess reserves (see the discussion on fractional reserve banking and the systemic debt-bias). It is recognized that there are periods of limited supply of credit, particularly during so-called "credit crunches" in which banks may have sustained loan losses leading to a contraction of credit; however, the underlying reason for the losses and contraction must be examined first; a contributing factor is likely to be the previous over-lending and excessive availability of credit earlier in the cycle.

Third, the debt service coverage ratio, which is already in common use by banks (particularly in real estate financing), places a constraint on lending that may be unappealing from the standpoint of credit expansion and meeting loan goals.

14

In sum, credit-based interest rates are believed to be a valuable reference because the interest rates computed embody the information about the *debt service capacity* of economic entities, with the essential assumption that debts are *paid in full*. Moreover, the computations are based on observable phenomena and Generally Accepted Accounting Principles (GAAP).

Finally, it may be of particular interest to compare the credit-based interest rates by firms and sectors to intuit prevailing economic conditions as well as to identify the emergence of any significant deviations from policy interest rates.

Note: Calculation Methods. Simple interest, compound interest, 360-day or 365-day interest accruals are not interest rates, but involve methods of calculating interest.

PART II

INTEREST RATE DETERMINATION: A HISTORICAL PERSPECTIVE

This section presents a cursory overview of thought on interest rate determination spanning the 18th, 19th, 20th and 21st century beginning with Adam Smith's 1776 magnum opus, *The Wealth of Nations*: *An Inquiry into the Nature and Causes of the Wealth of Nations*.

18th Century: Adam Smith

Profit and Interest Rates

Adam Smith's 1776 treatise *An Inquiry into the Nature and Causes of the Wealth of Nations* discusses interest rate determination in the context of the world of commerce. Smith is quite clear on a relationship between interest rates and profits. Comments and reflections are added in italics here although it is recommended that additional references on the writings of Adam Smith be consulted. Smith's definitions are provided below:

Profit. "The (revenue) derived from *stock*, by the person who manages or employs it, is called profit." (Smith, Book I: 59, Cannan Ed., 1976) *The term "revenue" could also be referred to as income.*

Interest. "That (revenue) derived from it (stock) by the person who does not employ it (stock) himself, but lends it to another, is called the interest or the use of money. It is the compensation which the borrower pays to the lender, for the profit which he has an opportunity of making by the use of the money." (Book I: 59)

Stock and Financing. From a financial standpoint, the term "stock" is assumed here to refer to a category of short-term working capital assets which could be cash/money or goods inventory. The term "stock" is introduced in the context of land, labor and stock elsewhere: "Whoever derives his revenue from a fund which is his own, must draw it either from his labour, from his stock, or from his land."(Book I, 59). *The term "stock" may later have been renamed to "capital." For the purpose of discussion below "stock" will be considered a short-term asset such as inventory.*

The section on interest appears to refer to trading activities and trade debt. "Stock" and money are treated similarly since money can be lent to purchase "stock" and "stock" itself can be "lent" (sold on credit) in the case of vendor financing. The repayment of principal is not mentioned here; in such a case, vendor financing would be applicable: The vendor lends to its customer by selling its stock on credit, generating a receivable; depending on the terms of the agreement, this receivable could be an interesting-bearing "account receivable" or "note receivable" held by the lender and a "trade payable" or "note payable" to the borrower. When the "stock" is sold (presumably at a profit) and the cash from the sale is collected by the borrower, then the borrower can repay the debt to the vendor with interest. Interest is charged until the receivable is collected; in a sense the interest may be thought of as a form of profit sharing (see below for Smith's discussion on "double interest").

16

Source of Interest. "Part of that profit naturally belongs to the borrower, who runs the risk and takes the trouble of employing it; and part to the lender, who affords him the opportunity of making this profit." (Book I: 59)

Market rate of interest internationally. "The market of rate of interest varies in any country....We may be assured that the ordinary profits of stock must vary with it, must sink as it sinks, and rise as it rises. The progress of interest, therefore, may lead us to form some notion of the progress of profit."(Book I, 99)

The interest rate and profit ("double interest"). It is apparent that a ratio between profit and interest was common knowledge at the time. Smith writes:

"Double interest is in Great Britain reckoned, what the merchants call a good, moderate, reasonable profit; terms which I apprehend mean no more than a common and usual profit. He states "In a country where the ordinary rate of clear profit is eight or ten percent, it may be reasonable that one half of it should go to interest, whenever business is carried on with borrowed money." (Smith, 1976: Book I: 109)

Smith also points out that in countries where the ordinary rate of profit is much higher or much lower, the *proportion* between interest and clear profit may change.

"Clear profit" may refer to the net profit.

Other Factors Affecting Interest Rates

Contract enforcement. A remarkable observation that higher interest rates can result from *risk of loss*, in particular in poor or unreliable enforcement of contracts:

"A defect in the law may sometimes raise the rate of interest considerably above what the condition of the country, as to wealth or poverty, would require. When the law does not enforce the performance of contracts, it puts all borrowers nearly upon the same footing with bankrupts or people of doubtful credit in better regulated countries. The uncertainty of recovering his money makes the lender exact the same usurious interest which is usually required from bankrupts."(Book I: 106)

Policy (legal) interest rates. Smith also writes of the Edict of 1766 in which the legal rate of interest was reduced from 5% to 4% (Book II, 380).

Protectionism. "A country which neglects or despises foreign commerce…cannot transact the same quantity of business which it might do with different laws and institutions." (Book I: 106)

Monopoly profits for the politically connected. "In a country too, where though the rich or owners of large capitals enjoy a good deal of security…the oppression of the poor must establish the monopoly of the rich, who, by engrossing the whole trade to themselves, will be able to make very large profits. Twelve percent, accordingly it is said to be the common interest of money in China, and the ordinary profits of stock must be sufficient to afford this large interest." (Book I: 107)

Interest rate declines and asset inflation. In an early reference to land bubbles, Smith mentions a relationship between land prices and interest rates, comparing England and France: "At 10% land was sold at for 10 and 12 years purchase. As interest sunk to 6, 5 and 4% the price of land rose to 20, 25 and 30 years purchase. The market rate of interest is higher in France than in England, and the common price of land is low. In England it commonly sells at 30, in France at 20 years purchase." (Book II, 380)

19th/ early 20th Century

Profit and Equilibrium Interest Rate

The work of Knut Wicksell (1898) on interest rates is summarized by Wilhelm Ropke (1936) in the following passages. On the monetary theory of the cycle, Ropke refers to "…the real rate of interest in Wicksell's sense or the equilibrium rate…." The "…equilibrium rate in the economic system which is only a fictitious figure reflecting roughly the average rate of profits anticipated from capital investment…." He also refers to the term "subjective real rate of interest" as "average profit expectation." (1936:114-115)

Ropke mentions this equilibrium rate in the context of cycles of boom and bust. It is worth providing Ropke's full text in which Wicksell is referenced is presented below (italics and a paragraph separation are added for emphasis):

Two key points highlighted are:

1. The equilibrium interest rate derives from expectations of a measure of profits on capital/capital investment;
2. Credit inflation arises from the widening of a gap between bank lending rates and the expected (or actual) profit on capital;

Insofar as the banks—led by the central note-issuing bank via its discount policy – lower or raise the rate of interest, there ensues an expansion or contraction of credit. The decisive factor is not the absolute height of the banks' interest rate, but the discrepancy between this and that rate of interest (the *real rate of interest in Wicksell's sense** or the *equilibrium rate*) which would establish itself if the volume of credit in the community were built up solely out of *real savings* and not out of *additional credits besides*.

A credit inflation can therefore very well arise by the very fact that the banks leave their interest rate unchanged or do not raise if far enough at a moment when the *equilibrium rate* in the economic system, which is only a fictitious figure reflecting roughly the *average rate of profits anticipated from capital investment*—has risen. This is, however, exactly what regularly happens in the boom period. If at the commencement of the boom the *profit expectations* of the economic system rise but the banks maintain their previous rate for credit advances or do not raise it sufficiently, then the automatic consequence is an increase in the demand for credit, owing to *the widening of the gap between the rate of interest and profits on capital.* In this case, therefore, no active intervention of the banks is necessary in order to call forth an increase in the demand for credit. It is sufficient if they do not follow or do not follow quickly enough the changes in *average profit expectations (subjective real rate of interest).* This is the situation that repeats itself with the beginning of every boom.

Wicksell's work has been revisited in the 21st century with some possible modifications to original definitions; the equilibrium interest rate is referred to as the natural interest rate. See the discussion on the 21st century below.

Time Preference Theory

The concept of time preference refers to people's general preference for obtaining things sooner rather than later. The role of time-preference in the determination of interest rates has been the focus of much research centering on the Austrian school of economics (Bohm-Bawerk 1901; Fetter 1914; Fisher 1907; Mund 1936; Rothbard 1990). Fetter (1914: 80-81) refers to time preference as a "rate of impatience."

While time preference might be considered to be a critical element in the analysis of interest rate determination, the difficulty of quantifying time preference and preference functions of individuals may have rendered its introduction into a framework for the determination of the real interest rate problematic for economists. A substitute for observation of time preference could be to observe realized real rates of return (Damodaran, 1996)

Capitalization Theory

Fetter (1914) in his exposition on capitalization theory, offers an explanation for the logic behind interest rates:

The productivity of which use is made when the explanation is really begun is not technical or physical productivity at all, but is the capacity which goods bought with judgment at current prices have, in the hands of enterprisers, of yielding a net surplus, sufficient not only to remunerate them, but to pay contract interest to lenders. The amount of interest which "enterprisers estimate" they can afford to pay…is the difference between the discounted, or present, worth of products imputable to these agents and their worth at the time they are expected to mature. The prices of the agents, which ae the costs, involve (not presuppose) a rate of discount. Fetter (1914: 86-98)

Here Fetter points to a link between "net surplus" or "value-surplus" or "rates of profit" and the interest rate. Also see Rothbard (1975:18).

The Hotelling Rule

In research on the economics of exhaustible resources, Harold Hotelling (1925, 1931) provides an important contribution, and may have relevance to other forms of economic activity. The *Hotelling Rule* as it has come to be known, states that "...the real price of an exhaustible resource, net of marginal extraction costs, must grow at a rate equal to the rate of interest..." (Devajaran 1981; Miller and Upton 1985). The equation is:

$$p_t = p_0 e^{rt}$$

Where p_t is "...interpreted as the net price received after paying the cost of extraction and placing upon the market, p_0 is the price in the initial period, and r is the rate of interest. Hotelling (1931:141). This equation could be reworded as "net profit grows at the rate of interest." The reader is also referred to Gray (1914). Miller and Upton (1985) conduct an empirical test of the Hotelling valuation principle for the U.S. oil and gas industry.

An immediate observation might be that exhaustible resource development offers an inappropriate comparison to other economic activity and in particular the macro-economy. However, it is not clear whether exhaustible resources such as oil can be considered to be entirely exhaustible, given the long periods over which they have been exploited and are expected to continue in production (Friedman 1996:170)

The major reason for introducing Hotelling's research is to highlight another example of some form of theoretical relationship between the rate of interest and the rate of growth in profits in an industry, as seen by an increase in the cost (price) from acquisition to the selling price.

20th Century: Transition to Macroeconomic Management

An interesting transition occurred in the 20th century, in which the research began to move in the direction of examining policy impacts on interest rates, as well as centrally planned interest rates, referred to above as *policy interest rates*. The policies were fiscal and monetary policy; the central entities were generally national governments and central banks, which ultimately required some coordination in order to achieve various policy objectives. A dominant view emerged that government spending and debt can be used as a tool to stimulate economic activity and *aggregate demand*. It is also important to note that this modern approach appears to have replaced the pre-20th century determination of the real interest rate.

Replacement of the Real Interest Rate: Fisher Equation.

Part of the transition from the old school of interest rate theory appears to have been a replacement of the Wicksellian real interest rate.

The determination of real interest rates was explained by Fisher (1930) as "…the price which equates the supply and demand for capital. The supply depends on people's willingness to save—that is, postpone consumption. The demand depends on the opportunities for productive investment. (Fisher 1930 as cited in Brealey and Meyers, 1996:642).

In the new formulation of the real interest rate, the real interest rate is first derived by estimation of the *nominal* interest rate. The nominal interest rate is simply the real interest rate plus a measure of inflation. Fisher's eponymous equation begins with the nominal interest rate and then calculates the real interest rate by subtracting the inflation rate from the nominal interest rate as follows:

$$r_t = m_t - \dot{p}_t$$

…where rn_t is the nominal interest rate and p_t(dot) is the inflation rate during the period t .

Because the nominal interest rate is adjusted for by a measure of inflation, the Fisher approach to determining the real interest rate drops the classical link between profit/returns and the real interest rate. The interest rate now can be estimated with the use of macro-econometric and other models with policy variables as the driving force. This is explained in the section below on interest rates in the context of the IS-LM framework

Competing Measures of Inflation.

The determination of the Fisherian version of real interest rate requires a measure of inflation. As of the 20th and 21st century, there are a wide variety of commonly-used measures for the inflation rate, including the percentage change in an index of prices such as the CPI, WPI or the GDP deflator and methodologies including the introduction of *hedonics*.

It is interesting to note other measures of inflation that no longer figure prominently in the common framework for inflation measures:

1. Incorporation of asset prices.

The Bank for International Settlements refers to "real aggregate asset prices" in its 1995-6 Annual Report as a composite measure of stock prices, residential real estate prices, and commercial real estate prices (cited by Grant 1996:310). At one time, the Snyder Index of the general price level incorporated asset prices (real estate and stock prices) (Rothbard, 1975:150).

2. Inflation defined as money and credit

Inflation has also been associated not with the general price level but rather, with the supply of additional quantities of money and credit to the economic system (cited by Grant 1996:298-299, 130). For the discussion on the similar topic of *currency dilution*, see the Appendix.

Interest Rates in the Context of the IS-LM Framework

The interest rate appears in the IS and the LM curve of the traditional Hicksian IS-LM framework or a suitable variant (Dornbusch and Fischer 1984). The IS curve shows national income as a function of government expenditures, the interest rate and autonomous taxes. The LM curve shows national income being a function of the money supply and the interest rate. The equilibrium interest rate can be solved for by equating these two curves as follows:

$$r_0 = \frac{-\phi(\alpha + \beta\tau + \zeta) - \phi g_t + [1 - \beta(1 - \varepsilon)](ms_t - \lambda)}{\phi\theta + \varphi[1 - \beta(1 - \varepsilon)]}$$

In this 20th century formulation, the equilibrium interest rate is a function of *autonomous taxes, government expenditures* and the *money supply*. This essentially sets the stage for the macro-economy to be managed by fiscal and monetary policy tools.

For the simple closed economy simultaneous equation macroeconomic model from which the above equilibrium interest rate equation is derived, as well as the subject of interest rates and crowding out in the IS-LM framework, see the Appendix and Kennedy (1999).

It should be noted that this formulation of the equilibrium interest rate appears to replaces the previous one defined by Wicksell and Ropke noted above and like the Fisher equation, also appears to remove any apparent link between profit/returns and the interest rate.

21st Century: Extensions of Interest Rate Estimation

The work of Knut Wicksell on the *natural interest rate* (NRI) (alternatively referred to as the *equilibrium interest rate*) remains of interest to monetary authorities and economic researchers into the 21st century.

Citations from Wicksell (1898) suggest the desirability of a certain neutrality of interest rates with respect to prices and the real economy:

"There is a certain rate of interest on loans which is neutral in respect to commodity prices, and tends neither to raise nor to lower them. (1898: 102 as cited in Manrique and Marques 2004, Laubach and Williams, 2003).

Wicksell had offered advice for monetary policy:

"So long as prices remain unaltered the [central] banks' rate of interest is to remain unaltered. If prices rise, the rate of interest is to be raised; and if prices fall, the rate of interest is to be lowered...." (1898: 189 as cited in Manrique and Marques 2004)

The 21st century determination of the natural interest rate lies within a macroeconomic framework. The natural interest rate (NRI) is now estimated with the aid of macroeconomic models.

Lundvall and Westermark (2011) offer a more modern definition of the *natural interest rate* as the real *equilibrium interest rate* independent of actual bank interest rates, determined by the real disturbances affecting the economy. A central bank wishing to hold prices stable would keep bank interest rates in line with the natural interest rate. The term "Neo-Wicksellian" model is occasionally used interchangeably with the "New Keynesian" model (Lundvall and Westermark, 2011).

Laubach and Williams (2003) define the natural rate to be the real Fed Funds rate with adjustments reflecting potential GDP, and the NRI is estimated based on movements in GDP. The model suggests that differences between the real Fed Funds rate and the natural rate can produce contractionary (*ffr>nri*) or stimulative (*ffr<nri*) effects, on GDP.

In sum, a comparison and contrast of the modern approach to the NRI with Wicksell's original exposition might be summarized as follows:

1. The equilibrium interest rate (natural interest rate or NRI) no longer derives from profits on capital/capital investment but from fluctuations in the macro-economy.
2. A widening of a gap between bank lending rates and the re-defined equilibrium interest rate is recognized as having an impact on national income (the topic of credit inflation may be outside the present framework).

Note: Ropke refers to "real interest rates" or alternatively the "equilibrium interest rate" in his overview of Wicksell's work (1936:114). 21st century references cited here refer to the equilibrium interest rate and the natural interest rate interchangeably, but real interest rates are not noted in the same context.

PART III

CREDIT-BASED INTEREST RATES

The previous historical overview suggests that there are two basic approaches to the determination of interest rates, one that relates interest to some measure of profit and profitability in an investment sense, and one that estimates interest within the context of the macro-economy as defined within the national income accounting framework. The shift from the former to the latter approach appears to have occurred beginning in the early 20th century. At present the macroeconomic determination of the real interest rate appears to be dominant.

The credit-based approach to interest rate determination centers on debt service coverage analysis. This credit-based approach computes, rather than estimates, the interest rate using a standard annuity formula. While the focus here is on business lending, the analysis could be applied to other entities as well as borrowing requests for individuals.

Firms, the Macro-economy and National Income Accounting

National income accounting is a highly specialized field and the following discussion on national income accounting is only a brief and rough overview for reference purposes. Nevertheless, the essential point, that national income accounting has a basis in microeconomic business activity, is considered to be valid.

The current approach to the determination of interest rates emphasizes broad macroeconomic factors to evaluate the impact of policies and policy tools. This generally requires some form of estimation usually with the aid of macro-economic models, rather than direct computation.

It may initially appear that a shift towards more microeconomic firm-level approach is irrelevant to determining interest rates. However national income accounting is essentially based on a firm-level accounting of the economy with its aggregation of business data. This business basis for national accounts may not be entirely obvious because of a general tendency to emphasize a *demand-side approach* to national income accounting; for further commentary on this subject, see the Appendix.

In the U.S., recent revisions in reporting by the Bureau of Economic Analysis' (BEA) may provide additional data to improve the understanding of business production. (Howells and Morgan, BEA, 2014)

Since the macro-economy is assumed to be fundamentally composed of businesses and microeconomic activity, the next step in this analysis is to clarify some basics of credit in the financing of firms, and the determination of interest rates in such a context.

Debt Service Coverage: Introduction

In credit analysis, a simple metric of the capacity of a firm to service its debt is the *debt service coverage* (DSC) ratio. Credit-based determination of the interest rate relies on this DSC ratio and an understanding of the factors underlying debt service coverage. A more detailed commentary on business credit is beyond the scope of this section is provided in the Appendix. Many outside resources on the fundamentals of credit analysis can be referred to as well.

The *debt service coverage* (DSC) ratio is defined as:

$$SOR / DS$$

...where the numerator SOR is the *primary source of repayment* for the loan. For the purposes of debt service coverage analysis, unless otherwise indicated, SOR is taken to mean *primary* SOR. (*Alternative* sources of repayment should be noted as such and are discussed below). The primary SOR has many possible definitions and depends on the preference of the analyst; the best approximation for the primary SOR is noted here with supporting explanations in the Appendix.

The denominator, DS refers to *debt service* which is defined as the sum of principal and interest (P+i). When principal repayments are not being made (as in interest-only payments, non-amortizing loans) P can be zero. More discussion on debt service is found below.

The figures for both SOR and DS should cover the same time period, such as monthly, quarterly or annually, depending on the analysis.

Primary Source of Repayment
The ability to service debt is assumed to originate from the firm's *internal, essential and recurring operations*, and can be referred to as the *primary source of repayment* (Primary SOR). There are a number of traditional measures of the primary SOR, including *net profit, net cash from operations*, and *funds flow*, and the general term "cash flow" which is often used without a clear definition. None of these are viewed as a satisfactory primary SOR. **NCF less dividends/distributions.** The best approximation of the primary source of repayment is *net cash flow* (NCF*) less dividends/distributions* with explanatory background provided in the Appendix. NCF alone is also referred to as free cash flow (FCF), and is generally defined as *net cash flow from operations* less *capital expenditures* (Capex). Further modifications can be made to NCF to provide an even more accurate measure for use as a primary source of repayment for debt, also noted in the Appendix.

For public firms dividends are deducted from NCF. For private firms and smaller businesses the firm may not pay dividends per se but may instead pay *owners' draws* or *distributions*. In all cases, dividends, distributions, owners' draws or other similar reductions of firm retained earnings are not generally assumed to be part of the primary SOR available to service the debt.

Debt Service Coverage and Capacity.

Debt Service is the sum of principal and interest (p+i) in a loan payment and is the amount of cash to be paid periodically (monthly, quarterly, annually) to repay a loan. The periodic amount of debt service depends on the principal balance of the loan, the interest rate, the *amortization period* and the *term (maturity) of the loan* (if the amortization matches the term/maturity then the loan is *fully amortizing*. A loan that does not amortize may be only *interest-bearing*.

Debt service coverage (DSC) is often expressed as a ratio such as 1.5. The lower the DSC ratio, theoretically the more risk that borrower cannot cover the debt service. When evaluating credit, the lender must decide an appropriate debt service coverage ratio for a particular borrower.

A comprehensive credit analysis requires an evaluation of how *consistently* the primary source of repayment is likely to cover debt service. This requires that the primary source of repayment be *recurring*. Significant variability in the primary SOR may be expected in the natural course of business and that should factor into the credit decision and an acceptable DSC ratio. Greater variability in cash flow would be expected to require a greater cushion; that is, the minimum DSC ratio might need to be raised. To avoid possible errors in estimating variability see the comments on probability theory and the assumption of normality in the Appendix.

Alternative sources of repayment. If a company's primary SOR for debt becomes insufficient to service the debt, from the creditor's standpoint (e.g. bank, bondholder, investor), the risk of default on the loan can be viewed as more likely. Reliance on *alternative* sources of repayment to service debt, such as additional debt accumulation or equity issuance may result in future burdens on the company, the investors, or result in untimely asset liquidations. Debt restructuring may eventually be necessary to better match the entity's cash flow to debt service requirements.

Computing the Credit-Based Interest Rate

The credit-based approach solves for the interest rate that conforms to a given debt service coverage (DSC) ratio and loan term. This is significant because the interest rate computed contains the information about the creditworthiness of the borrower in relationship to a *full payoff* of the debt.

The following chart shows the overall relationship between the loan term with matching amortization (i.e. fully amortizing), the debt service coverage ratio (1.25 – 2.0) and the interest rate that is computed from these criteria.

P/SOR. The chart below is for a *principal/source of repayment* (P/SOR) multiple of 4. This means that the principal balance of the loan is four times greater than the annual primary source of repayment amount. Source of repayment is defined as *NCF less dividends/distributions* as discussed above.

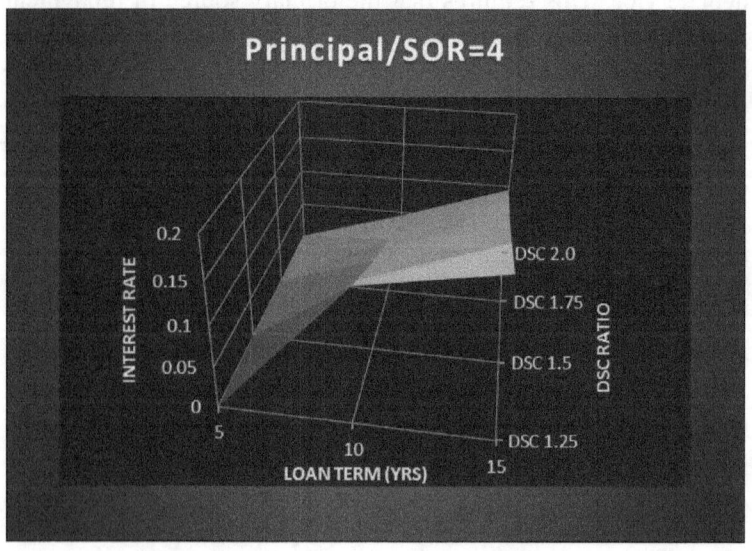

Full amortization. To ensure that the debt is fully paid off, full amortization of the loan is required and therefore the amortization period must match the term/maturity of the loan. For example, a 10-year loan must have an amortization period of 10 years.

Note that many loans may mature before they fully amortize; (e.g. loans with a balloon whose terms are shorter than the amortization). Other loans do not amortize at all such as interest-only loans (including permanent non-amortizing lines of credit to be discussed).

Amortization period. The amortization period depends largely on what is being financed: Machinery, real estate, crops, etc. In theory the amortization is expected to correspond to the time period over which the primary SOR will remain sufficient to service the debt with appropriate coverage. For example, if financing is sought for equipment that has a usable life of say 7-10 years which would contribute an additional cash flow (adding to the primary SOR) of x amount for the business over 7-10 years then an amortization of 7 to 10 years might be a reasonable initial reference point. In addition, industry change and competition, early obsolescence and other considerations may need to be factored into the decision. Note that this is an example for a single loan for a single piece of equipment; for more complex financing requests analysis of the business' overall primary SOR and long-term debt service capacity of the borrowing entity would be necessary. For additional details on credit analysis and evaluation, see the Appendix.

Annuity formula: This credit-based approach solves for the interest rate that results in the maximum allowable periodic payment so as to conform to a given debt service coverage (DSC) ratio. The formula used is for the payment of an ordinary annuity:

$$PMT = r\,(P_0) \,/\, 1-(1+r)^{-n}$$

PMT is the periodic payment. The rate r is the interest rate for the loan, n is the number of periods of the payments, and the initial principal balance of the loan is P_0 (also often shown as PV or present value). Because the loan is assumed to be fully-amortizing there is no cash balance left over after the last payment and the future value (FV) is zero (i.e. no balloon). The payments are assumed to be made at the *end* of each period.

Example: A 10-year fully-amortizing loan of 100 currency units (say $U.S.) at 10% and with monthly payments. The annual interest rate of 10% is transformed to monthly as follows: 0.10/12, the number of periods is 120 (a 10-year loan with monthly payments = 10*12), and the amount of the loan (principal balance) is $100. The monthly payment should be approximately $1.32 (for the annual payment multiply by 12).

Computation procedure. This credit-based approach does not start with an interest rate, which must be computed. Popular software programs can be used for basic computations. When computing the credit-based interest rate, the annuity formula can be used in two stages: First the *maximum acceptable payment amount* is calculated for a given debt service coverage ratio (1.25, 1.5, 1.75, 2.0). Next, the interest rate that corresponds to this maximum acceptable payment amount is computed by trial-and-error (more complex programs can make the calculations by iteration).

Results: Interest rates at various P/SOR multiples. The following preliminary charts show interest rates that are computed at various DSC ratios (1.25, 1.5, 1.75 and 2.0) for fully amortizing loans of 5, 10 and 15 year terms for various P/SOR multiples. The title indicates the term and DSC Ratio. The SOR=1 relates to the horizontal axis titled "principal balance" meaning that a "principal balance" of 3 means *3x the annual SOR*, or alternatively stated, the P/SOR is 3.

A logarithmic trend line is added to the charts, but may be of limited value.

Computation Example

DSC=2, Term=15 Yr. (Annual NCF=1)

The debt service coverage (DSC) ratio in the chart is 2.0 (shown as DSC=2). A debt service ratio of 2.0 (shown as DSC=2) means that that the primary SOR must be twice the annual debt service amount (DSC=2 is the strictest debt service coverage ratio studied here). For a DSC ratio of 2.0 the *maximum allowable annual debt service amount* in currency terms is set at 0.5 currency units (for example, $ US 0.50) per year.

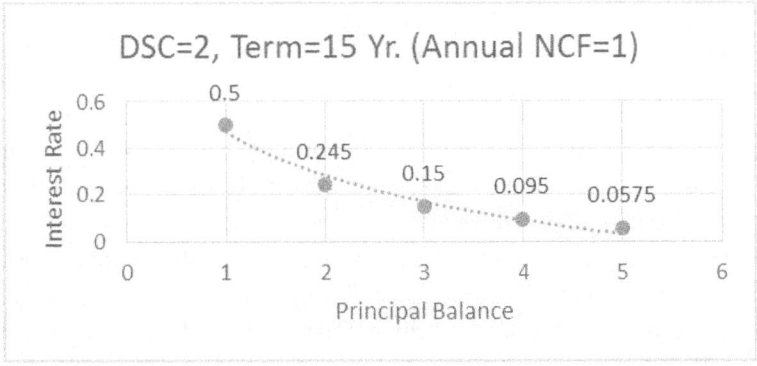

The horizontal axis titled "principal balance" shows figures 1 through 5. These figures indicate the principal balance as a *multiple* of the SOR and called the *principal to source of repayment multiple* or P/SOR multiple. Therefore, a figure of 3 in the horizontal axis means the principal balance of the loan is 3x the SOR, alternatively stated P/SOR=3.

Clarification: "Annual NCF=1" in the chart refers to the primary SOR in relation to the principal balance (on the horizontal axis). A source of confusion is that "annual NCF" was used for brevity in the chart but correctly stated should be *"annual NCF less dividends/distributions"* as explained in the above discussion defining the primary SOR). Thus, in relation to the principal balance figure "3" on the horizontal axis, the primary SOR is sized to 1.

Next, a term for the loan (5, 10 or 15 years, fully amortizing) is selected. Using a standard loan amortization formula as shown above for a 15-year term, fully amortizing, the interest rate that causes the debt service payment to equal exactly 0.5 currency units (for example $ US 0.50) at P/SOR=3 is shown as 0.15 or 15%. For P/SOR=4, the interest rate that results in the maximum debt service payment is 0.095 or 9.5% per annum.

Other Loan Terms: The focus of this study is business financing. Note that for fully-amortizing terms less than 5 years, it is exceedingly difficult for a firm to support a positive or even zero interest rate that can fully amortize the principal amount. There may of course be exceptions for highly profitable firms with relatively little debt in certain sectors.

For a term of 30 years, which is the term of many mortgages, the interest rate computed can be exceedingly high because the repayment is stretched out over a long period of time; a 30-year term is not shown here. Thirty years is considered to be less relevant to business financing and is not shown here. Typically, the target investments for which financing would be sought by businesses most likely would be obsolete (and no longer producing cash flow) well before 30 years' time. Real estate including land investments might be the exception, although terms may still tend to be shorter.

What may appear to be an error in the interest rate occurs at the lower levels of P/SOR. At P/SOR=1 or 2, the primary source of repayment is strong enough to service the debt at exceedingly high interest rates (up to 80%) especially at longer terms and lower DSC ratios.

DSC 1.25 (5, 10, 15)

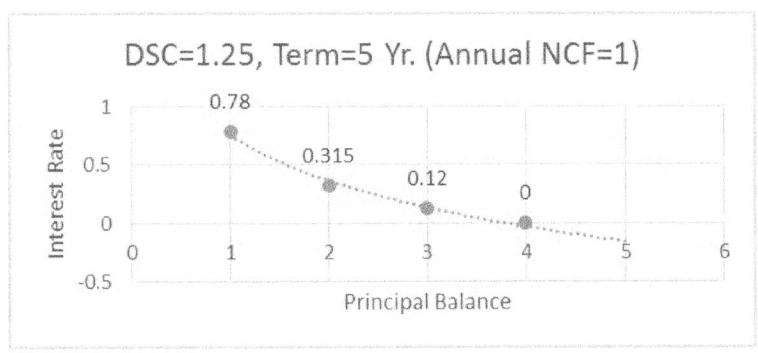

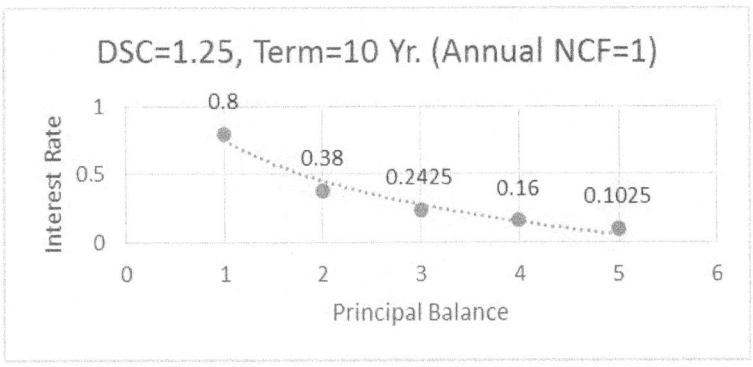

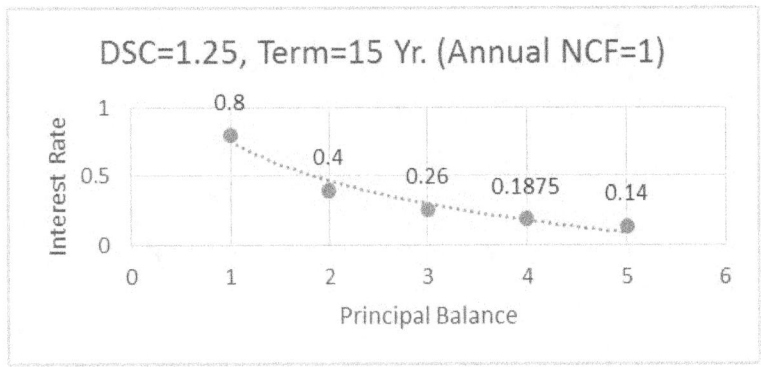

DSC 1.5 (5, 10, 15)

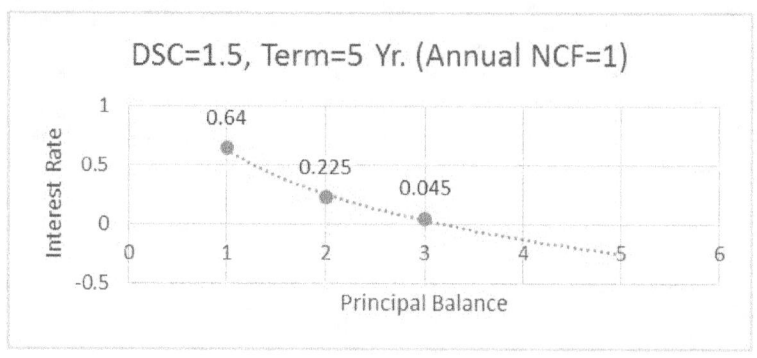

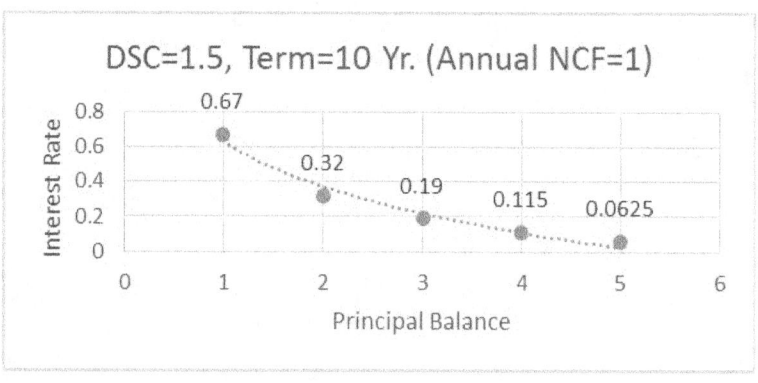

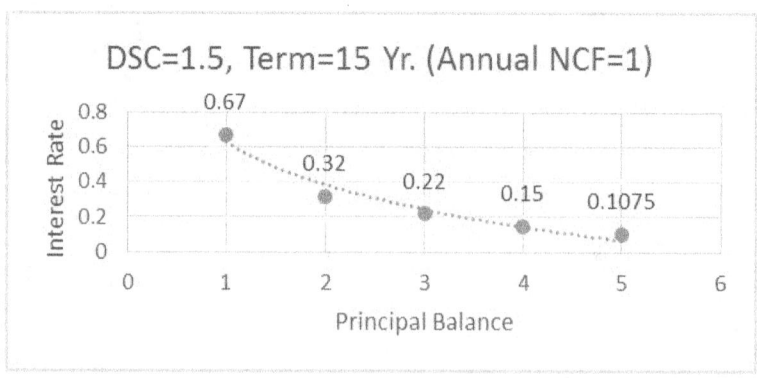

DSC 1.75 (5, 10, 15)

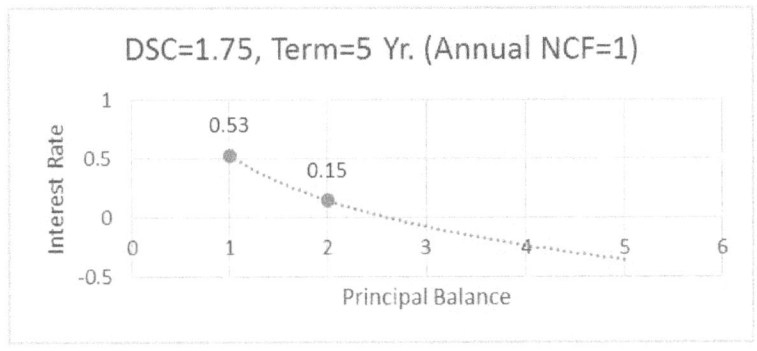

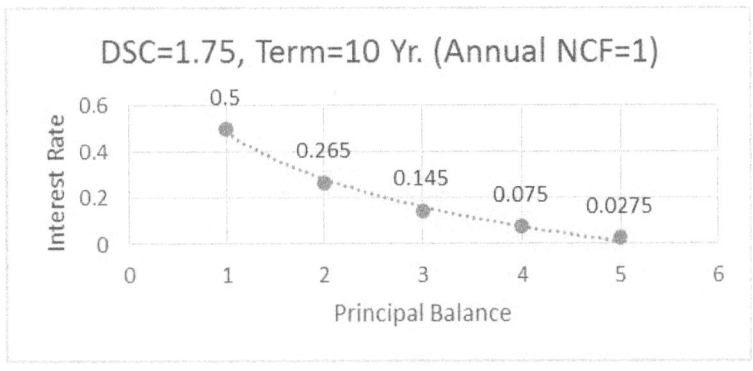

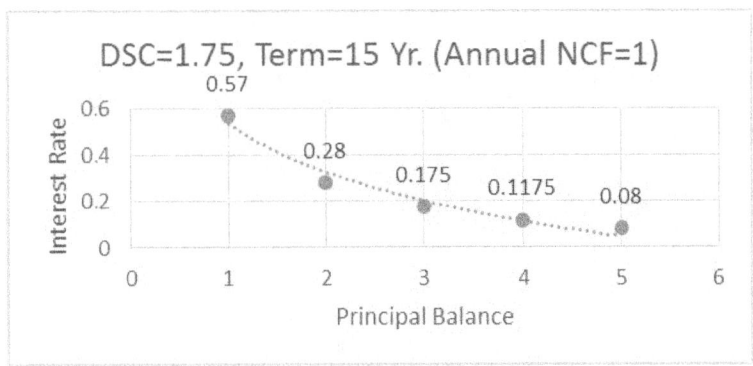

DSC 2.0 (5, 10, 15)

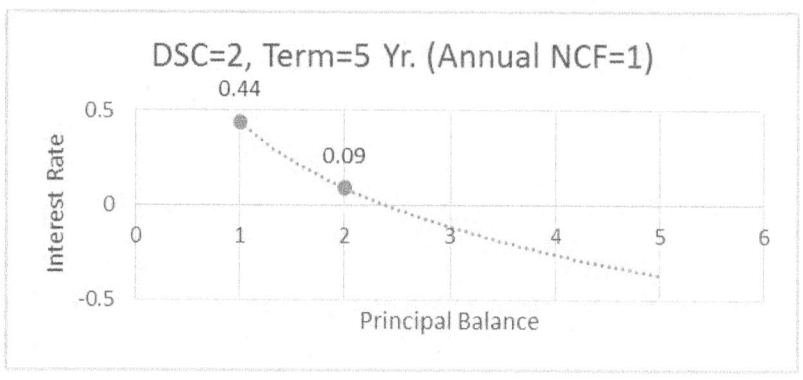

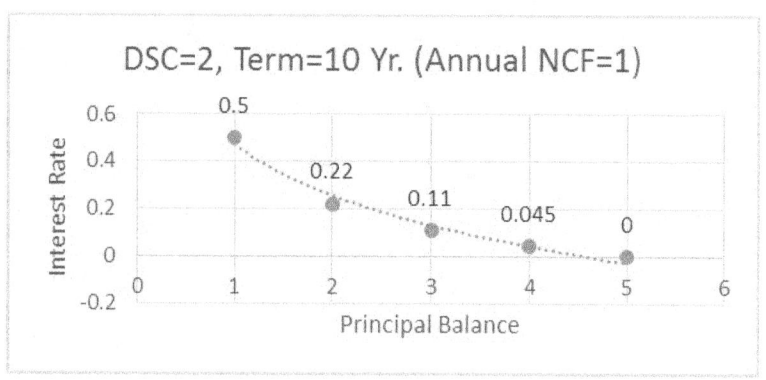

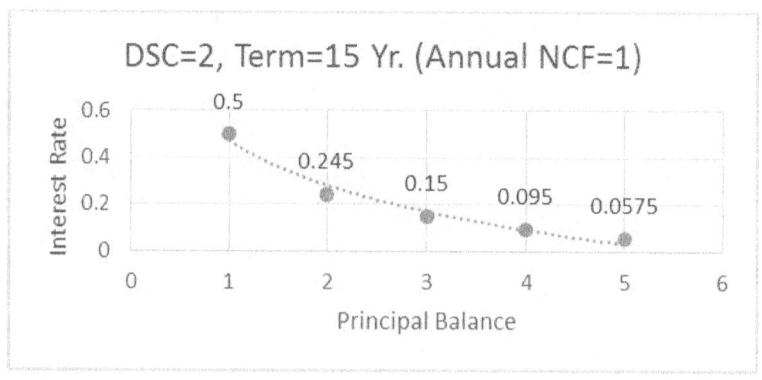

Commentary. Note that all economic entities are expected to have their own interest rate and no single "universal" interest rate can be said to exist because business cash flows vary from firm to firm and over time. In addition, an acceptable DSC can vary according to the lender's evaluation of the borrower's creditworthiness. However, a rough measure of interest rates by sector and subsector could be estimated for general reference taking into account issues with the normality assumption (see the section on probability theory in the Appendix).

SECTOR GROUPINGS AND RESULTS

Sample Data and Methodological Notes

Using the credit-based methodology presented herein, interest rates are computed for non-financial publicly-traded firms classified by sector with a total market capitalization of approximately US$500 billion as of 2014.

Sample Selection. Publicly-traded non-financial firms were selected for this study with some geographic diversification. Firms listed on either the NYSE or the NASDAQ have audited financial statements and filings with the U.S. Securities and Exchange Commission (SEC) which are expected to improve the quality of financial information. These filings are predominantly 20-F and 10-K reports.

The above criteria resulted in the sample excluding firms with less than $ U.S. 25B in market capitalization, as well as a concentration of sectors and subsectors.

Sectors. There are five sectors (*sector* is also often referred to as *industry*) with one subsector represented within each sector:

Basic Materials Sector: Independent Oil & Gas
Consumer Goods Sector: Beverages-Production & Distribution:
Healthcare Sector: Pharmaceutical
Technology Sector: Computer software: Prepackaged

Industrial Sector: Diversified Machinery

Distribution of Firms and Sectors
Geographic. The country refers generally to the legal jurisdiction of incorporation, as reported to the SEC. The firms selected were from Canada, Germany Israel, and the U.S.
Market Capitalization. The total market capitalization of the firms is estimated at $US $500 billion as of 2014.

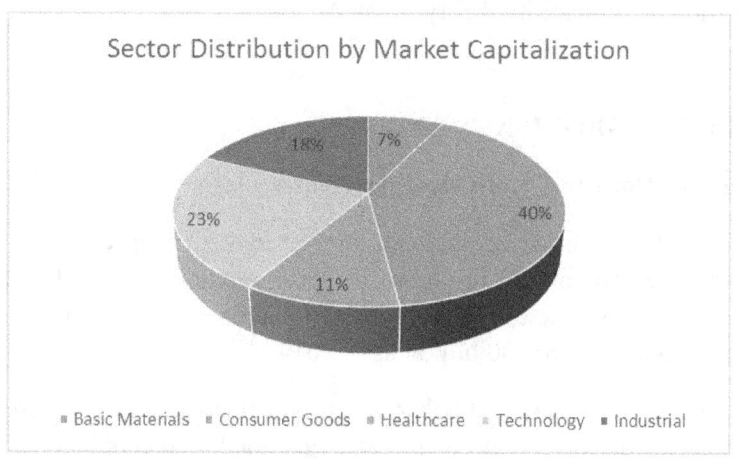

It is recognized that the consumer goods sector represents a disproportionate 40% of the total market capitalization, followed by technology (23%) and basic materials (18%).

Firm Identification. Primary. Due to the long-term likelihood of changes including mergers and acquisitions at which point certain names may be subsumed, the emphasis was placed on the sectors and subsectors in which the firms operate. Moreover, businesses can over time migrate from one subsector to another or straddle more than one subsector, as has been noted elsewhere. In addition, over time some subsectors may disappear in their current form in response to technological change, regulatory or other factors.

Financial Data

Source. The data are sourced from the financial statements of the selected firms in either their filings with U.S. Securities and Exchange Commission (SEC), which are typically the 20-F or 10-K Reports, or company annual reports that include the financial statements.

The financial statements are generally audited by one of the "Big 4" accounting firms (formerly known as the "Big 8"), Deloitte Touche, Pricewaterhouse Coopers, Ernst&Young, and KPMG, sometimes possibly in conjunction with a local accounting office, whether or not affiliated with one of the four firms.

For non-U.S. dollar currencies, the currency units used are local and are not converted into U.S. dollars.

Observation Period. The sample data were collected from the three fiscal years from 2011 to 2013 (calendar year basis.

Fiscal Year. Most firms report their financial information on a *calendar-year basis* i.e. for one year ending on December 31 of that year. For firms that report their financial information on another basis, the fiscal year is generally advanced by one year. For example, if ABC Inc.'s fiscal year ends on December 31st, 2013, the fiscal year is calendar year basis and is referred to as fiscal year 2013 (or abbreviated as FY 2013). If XYZ, Inc.'s fiscal year ends June 30th, 2014, XYZ's fiscal year is referred to as FY 2014.

Data Points. The original data needed for the computation of the interest rates are taken for each fiscal year are as follows (financial statement source indicated in bold):
Balance Sheet: Long term debt and short-term debt. Short-term debt includes CPLTD (current portion of long-term debt) and other debt.
Cash Flow Statement: Net cash from operations, capital expenditures and dividends.

41

Data Transformations
The above data for each fiscal year are transformed to create new variables representing the source of repayment (SOR), and the Principal-SOR Multiple.

The source of repayment (SOR) is *net cash flow less dividends* (NCF less dividends). There are two stages to the calculation of SOR: First, NCF is calculated by subtracting capital expenditures from *Net Cash from Operations*. Next, *NCF less dividends* is constructed by subtracting dividends from net cash from operations for each fiscal year.

Principal-SOR Multiple: The Principal-SOR multiple is computed by dividing the principal balance to be refinanced by the NCF less dividends from above.

It is initially assumed that the principal balance is all *long-term debt* of the firm, to be rolled into one loan and refinanced. In addition to long-term debt, it is likely that for many firms there is a significant portion of short-term debt that remains in the form of unamortized "permanent working capital" loans that should be amortized, as well. For a more comprehensive principal amount, a refinancing package including CPLTD and permanent working capital could also be considered. It is recognized that some firms may be unable to cover the debt service on such a larger amount, however.

Once the principal balance is identified and the Principal-SOR multiple is computed, the interest rate can be computed that fully amortizes the principal balance over the selected amortization term (10 or 15 years, matching the term) at a given debt service coverage ratio (1.25, 1.5, 1.75 or 2.0).

Linear interpolation: When the calculated interest rate fell in between two P/SOR ratios (such as 3 and 4), the interest rate was approximated by linear interpolation; this is recognized as only a rudimentary approximation.

42

Example of Interest Rate Computation

Assume that in fiscal year 2013 a firm's net cash from operations is 5817, capital expenditures 1665, dividends 1730, and long-term debt is 4296 (amounts are in millions, i.e. 5817 is 5,817,000,000). The primary source of repayment, NCF less dividends, is 2422 (5817-1665-1730 = 2422).

The Principal-SOR multiple is calculated by dividing 4296 by 2422, which is 1.77. Linear interpolation is used to estimate the interest rate between the Principal-SOR multiples of 1.0 to 2.0 with the shortcoming noted above. Hypothetical interest rate results are presented below for each term (fully amortized) and debt service coverage (DSC) ratio:

Loan Refinance, Term and Amortization (matching)	Debt Service Coverage (DSC)	Interest Rate
10-Year Term, Fully Amortized	DSC=1.25	3.8%
10-Year Term, Fully Amortized	DSC=2.0	0.0%
15-Year Term, Fully Amortized	DSC=1.5	9.5%
15-Year Term, Fully Amortized	DSC=2.0	4.7%

Explanation. The shorter the loan and amortization term the greater the source of repayment required to service the debt. The larger the debt service coverage ratio the more stringent the credit requirement is (a greater "cushion" is needed between the SOR and the debt service amount). Therefore, it is possible that for a particularly fast-amortizing and strict DSC ratio requirement, the only interest rate that the firm can "afford" to pay is 0%, as in the example above.

For companies that have a *negative* primary SOR, even a zero interest rate exceeds their debt service capacity, and a debt restructure may need to be considered.

Data Discrepancies. The terminology and composition of data may differ somewhat across firms. Although the financial information is considered to be of good quality, data discrepancies can occur and the composition of certain categories such as capital expenditures may not be uniform across firms. Financial statements are always subject to revisions in subsequent years. The data used are subject to revisions and may be updated from time to time.

RESULTS BY SECTOR

The charts below display the interest rates calculated for each fiscal year from 2011 to 2013 based on the actual financial data for the firms. If the results indicate that a firm cannot amortize the debt at any positive interest rate, including zero, the interest rate is a flat line at zero and below the chart is a qualifier: "debt restructure."

Charts are for a hypothetical DSC ratio of 1.5 (moderate level of leniency) and 2.0 (more stringent), for terms and matching amortizations (fully amortizing loans) of 10 and 15 years.

The principal balance for refinancing is long-term debt with two exceptions: Due to the financial strength of the firms in the last two sectors (technology and industrial goods), the principal balance of the refinancing includes both long-term and short-term debt.

It should be emphasized that although the interest rates are calculated for each fiscal year separately, this does not imply that the credit decision would necessarily be made annually for a refinance.

Nor does it imply that the credit-decision should be made on the basis of a single year of data. This exercise is simply to illustrate the various interest rates that result from the data for each fiscal year.

The credit decision should normally take into account a period of several fiscal years of the annual primary source of repayment amount, its variability and other factors. Then, an acceptable debt service coverage ratio can be decided upon. However, because of problems of assuming normality with financial data, particular care should be taken in selecting an appropriate DSC ratio. This topic requires further elaboration; for more on probability theory and issues concerning measures of dispersion such as the standard deviation, see the Appendix.

BASIC MATERIALS SECTOR (OIL)

10-year term and amortization (fully amortized)

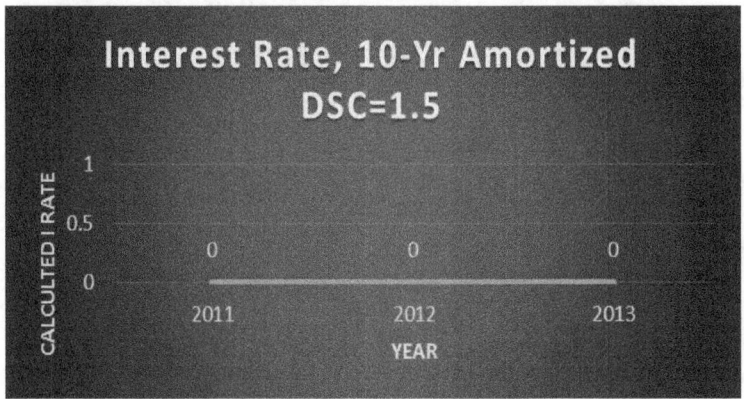

DEBT RESTRUCTURE

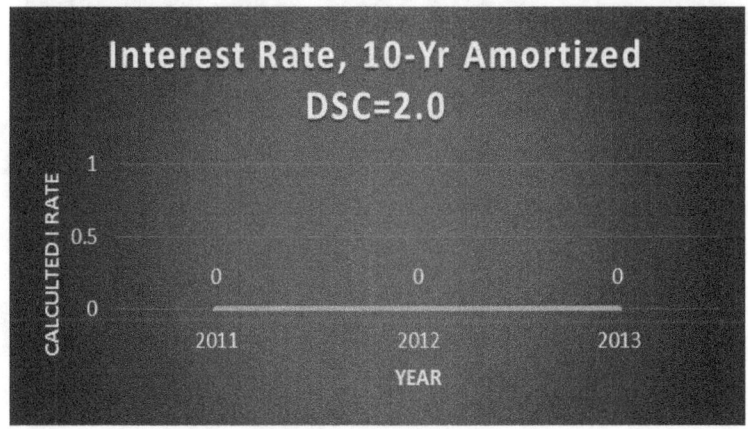

DEBT RESTRUCTURE

15-year term and amortization (fully amortized)

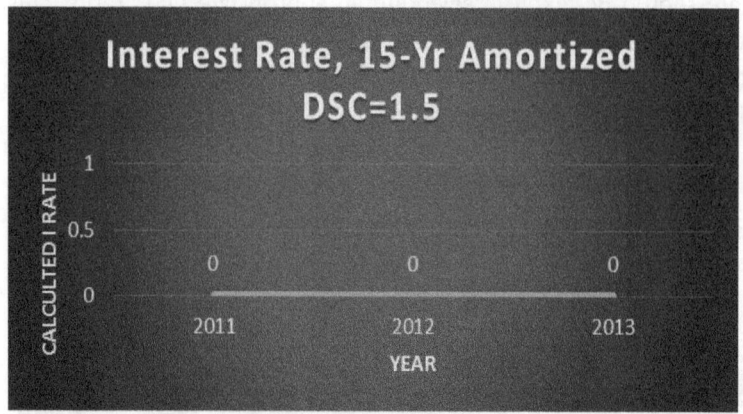

DEBT RESTRUCTURE

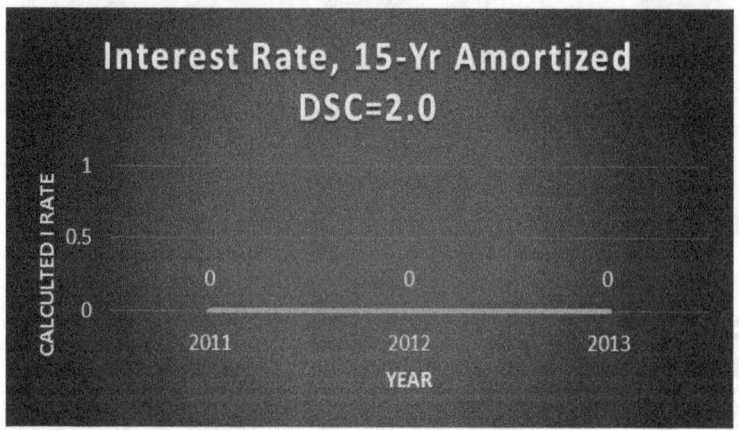

DEBT RESTRUCTURE

CONSUMER GOODS SECTOR

10-year term and amortization (fully amortized)

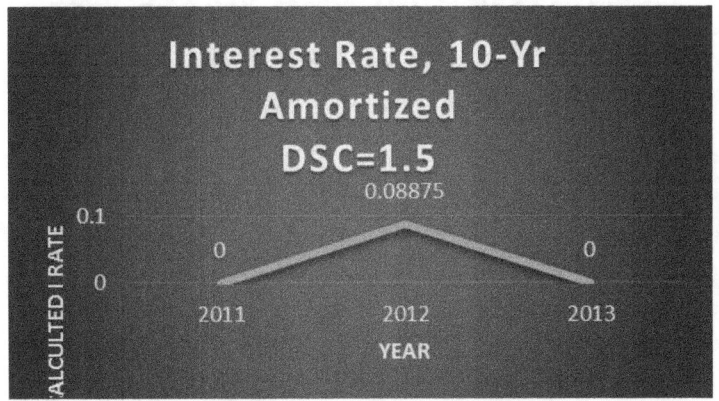

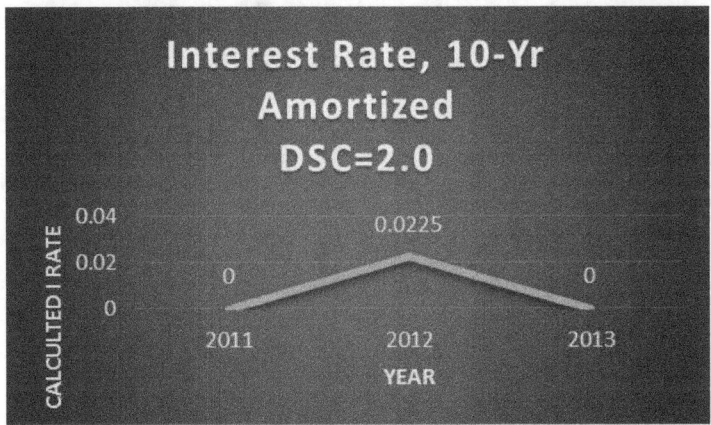

15-year term and amortization (fully amortized)

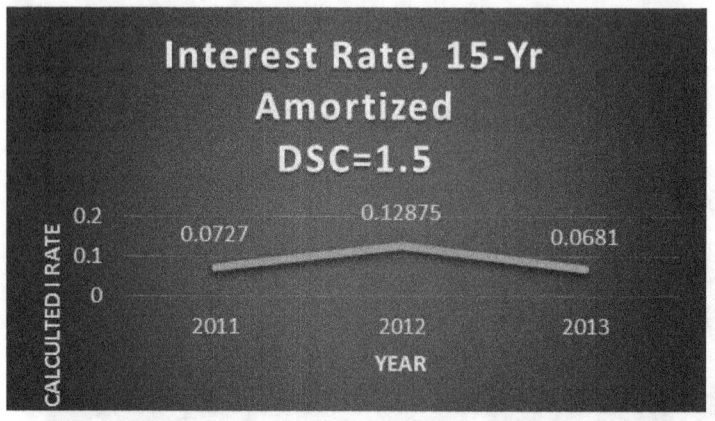

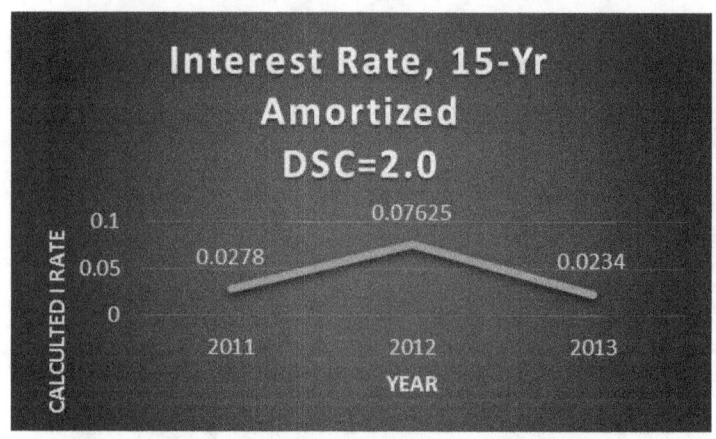

HEALTHCARE SECTOR

10-year term and amortization (fully amortized)

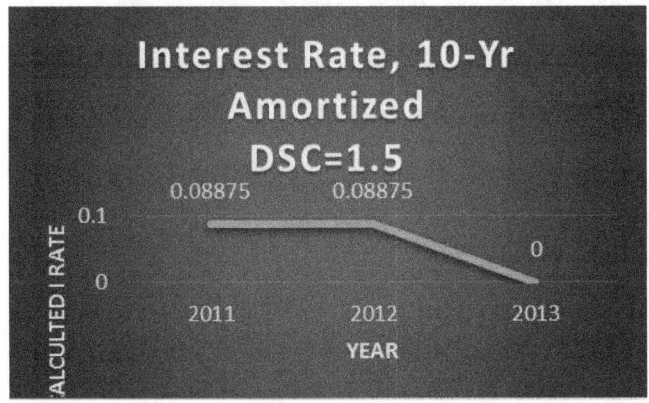

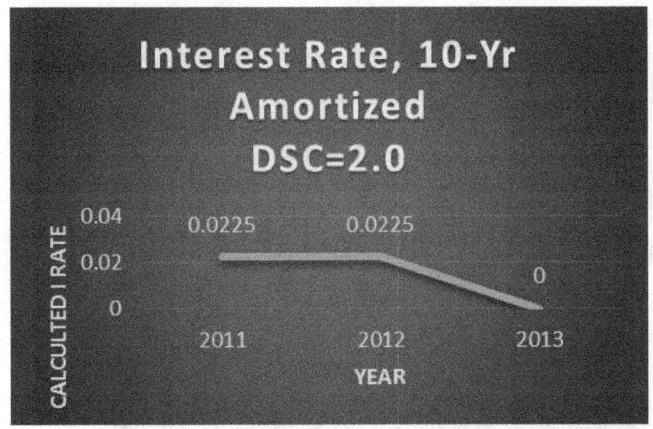

15-year term and amortization (fully amortized)

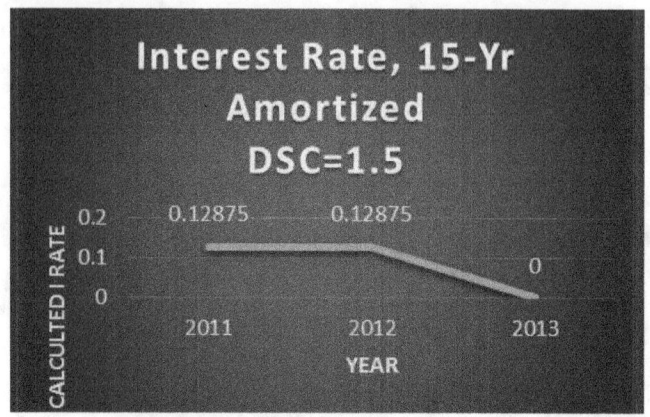

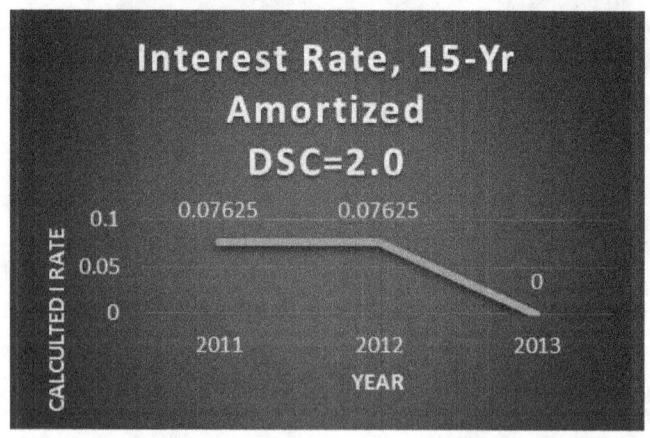

TECHNOLOGY SECTOR

10-year term and amortization (fully amortized)

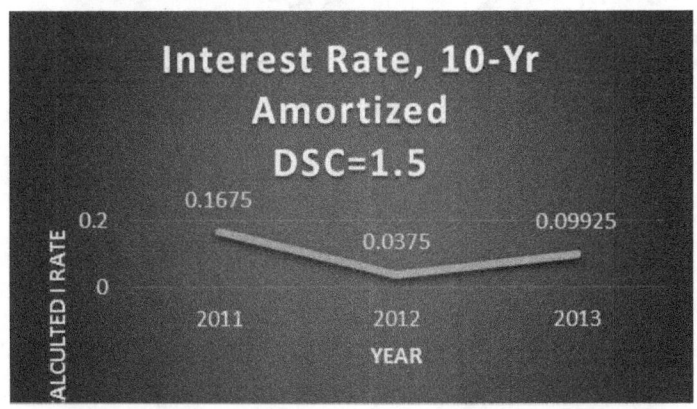

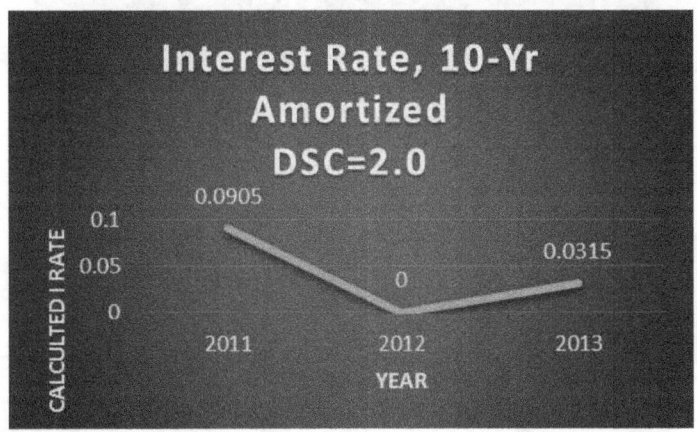

15-year term and amortization (fully amortized)

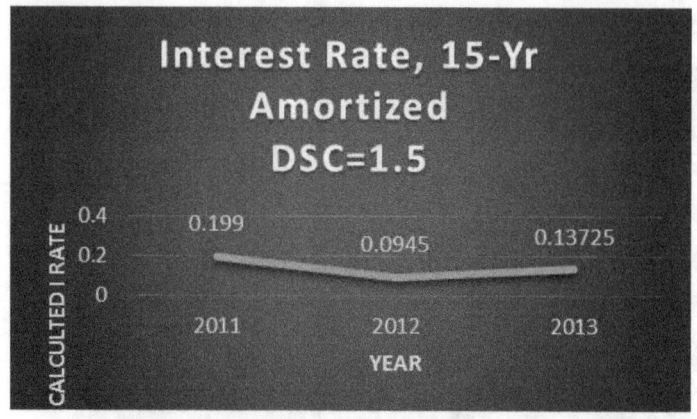

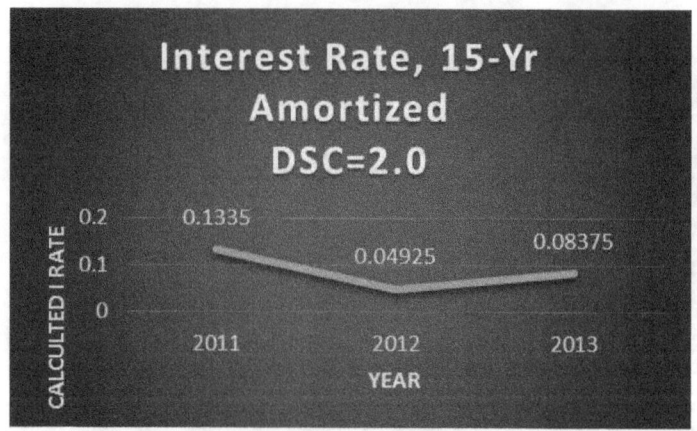

Note: *Due to the financial strength of the firm (i.e. high NCF-D), the principal balance refinanced includes both long-term debt and short-term debt.*

INDUSTRIAL GOODS SECTOR

10-year term and amortization (fully amortized)

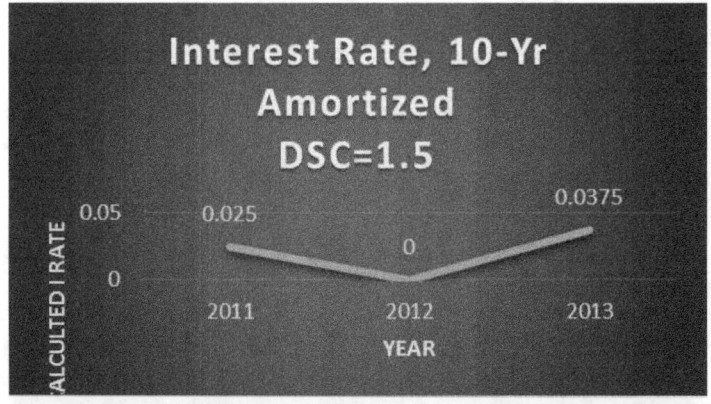

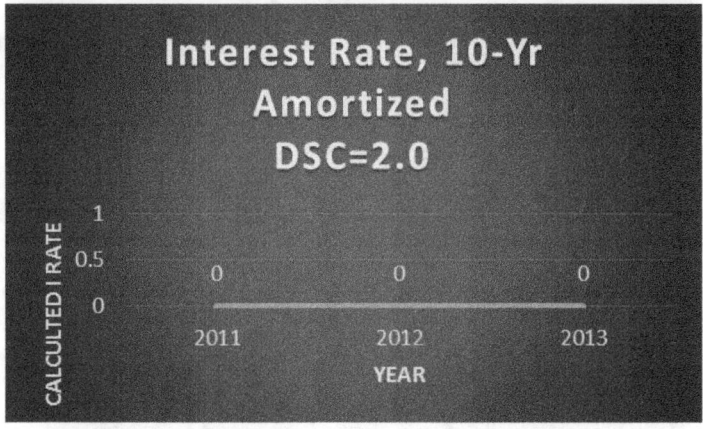

53

15-year term and amortization (fully amortized):

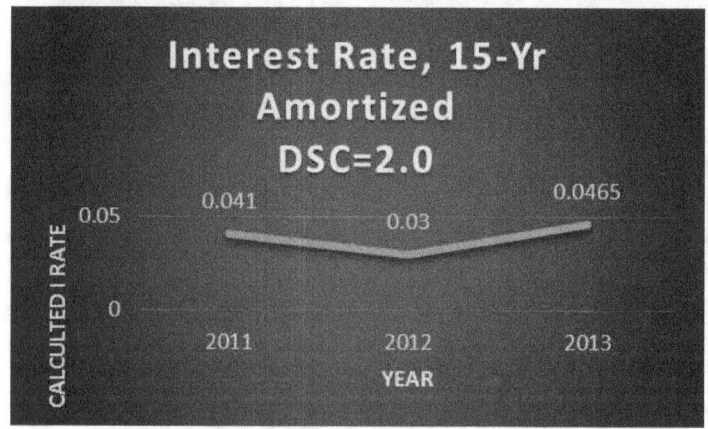

Note: *Due to the financial strength of the firm (i.e. high NCF-D), the principal balance refinanced includes both long-term debt and short-term debt.*

COMPARING RETURNS AND INTEREST RATES

Introduction

An interesting question for creditors and investors in debt is the *return* on debt instruments and loans with interest rates that appear to be identical.

This section compares the return of various types of debt with an identical initial principal balance of 100 currency units (US $100) and that carry the same apparent interest rate of 6% and term/maturity of 5 years (60 months).

The basis for comparison of returns is measured by the internal rate of return (IRR). For comparison with the IRR, the modified internal rate of return (MIRR), which accounts for financing costs and reinvestment, is used. The MIRR assumes a 6% annual reinvestment rate.

The five types of debt examined are as follows:

1. Permanent non-amortizing working capital *line of credit* (labelled permanent WC LOC)—this loan is assumed not to be paid off at the end of the 5 year period.
2. A zero coupon bond at 6%, maturing in 5 years.
3. A fully-amortizing 5 year term loan at a 6% stated rate, labelled "6% full amort."
4. A so-called "plain vanilla bond" of 6% with semi-annual payments, sold at par. See *yield measures* comment below. This bond is labelled "6% coupon semi-annual pmt."
5. The debt labelled "6% coupon monthly pmt" could be a bond that makes monthly interest payments to maturity. It also could represent a hypothetical *line of credit* as in (1) above but with the difference being that the line is pays interest every month and is *paid off in full* at the end of the 5-year term.

Yield measures. The question might arise as to the *yield* of the 6% coupon "plain vanilla" bond labelled. This bond is assumed to be sold *at par* so that the coupon rate of 6% is equal to the current yield (6%) and the yield to maturity (6%).

Redemption timing. The charts show the assumption that redemption/payoff is made with the final payment. Because the timing of the redemption/payoff can affect the return the difference was verified. Figures shown in the table below compare redemptions made with the final payment (month 60) and in the month after the final payment (month 61). The "permanent WC LOC" is omitted from the table as it is not paid off. For the zero coupon bond and the fully-amortizing loan the second case is marked not applicable (n/a): The zero coupon bond is assumed to be redeemed at month 60 with the interest payment, and the balance of the fully-amortizing loan is paid in full with the final payment in month 60.

Redemption Assumptions	Return	Mo pmt	Semi-ann	Full amort	Zero C
Made with final pmt	IRR	0.0600	0.0593	0.0600	0.0526
Made in mo after final pmt	IRR	0.0592	0.0584	n/a	n/a
Made with final pmt	MIRR	0.0600	0.0594	0.0600	0.0526
Made in mo after final pmt	MIRR	0.0593	0.0586	n/a	n/a

Results of Returns Analysis

For the results of the returns on the various debt instruments, please refer to the charts below. The color-coding of the charts may not reproduce well and details are provided with each chart.

IRR Comparisons

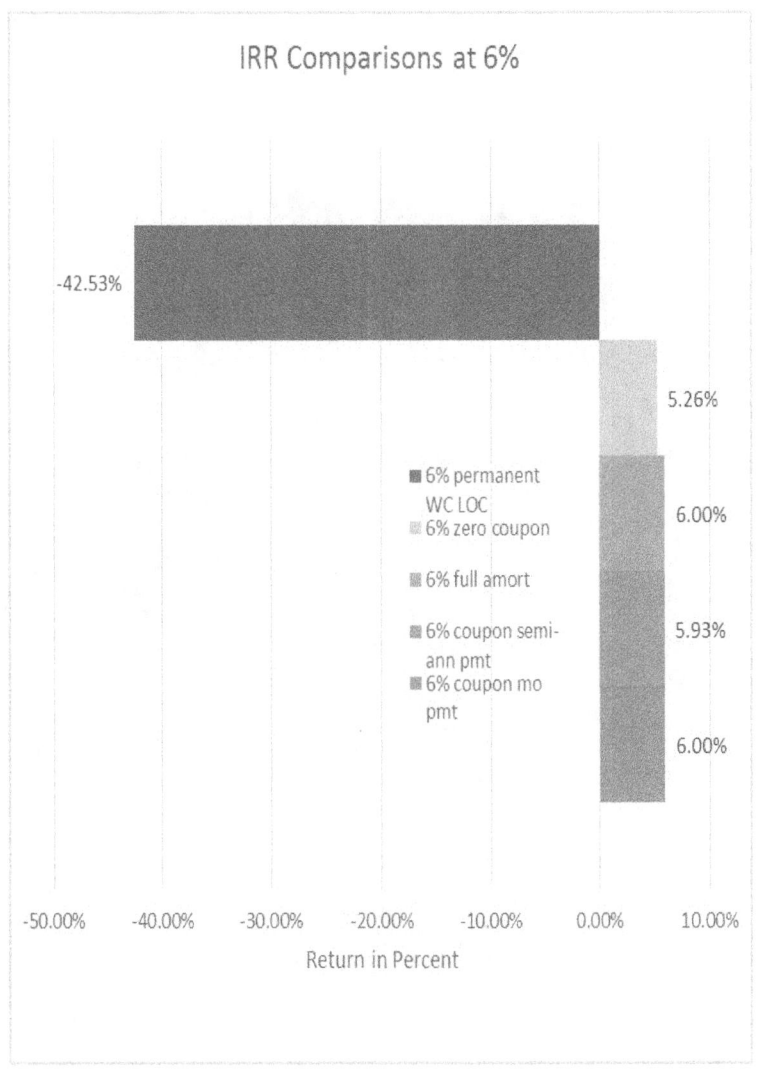

MIRR Comparisons

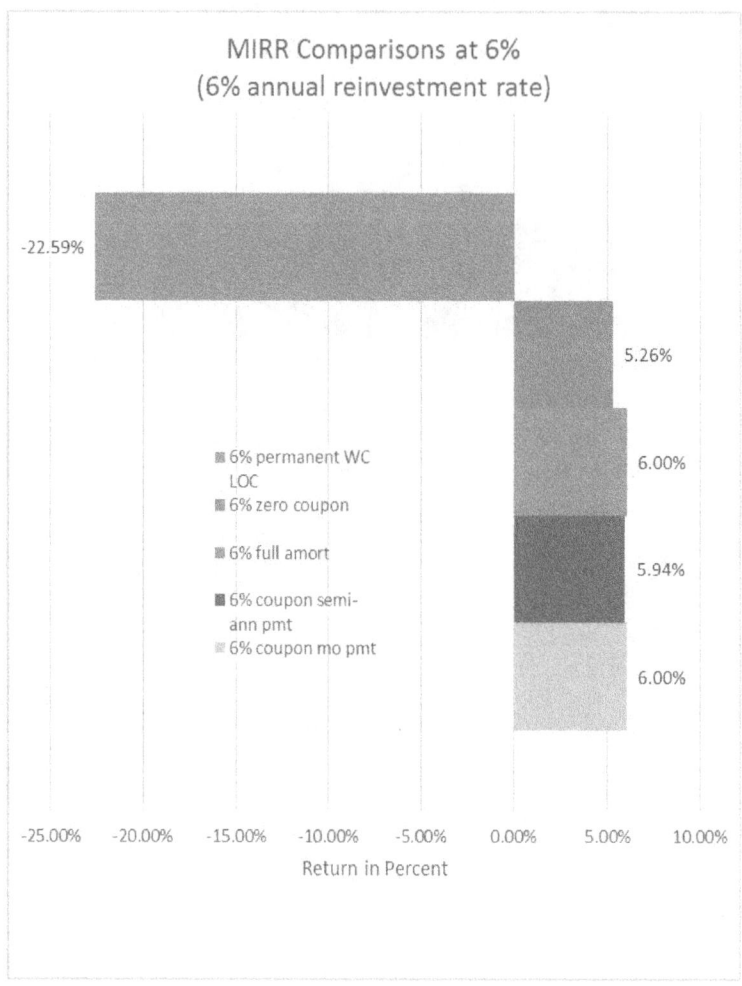

MIRR Comparisons at 6%
(6% annual reinvestment rate)

Summary of results. Comments are for the IRR results:

1. Permanent non-amortizing working capital line of credit (labelled permanent WC LOC): Negative 42% return. This investment the worst-performing of all debt instruments as it does not pay off at maturity.

2. A zero coupon bond: 5.26%. Note the significant difference between the stated 6% rate of the zero coupon bond and this calculated IRR.
3. Fully-amortizing 5 year term loan: 6%
4. The plain vanilla bond: 5.93% (slightly below 6%)
5. The 6% coupon monthly payment: 6%. Because the line is paid off at maturity, the return is restored to 6%.

Comparison of Cash Flow Timing

The chart below shows how various types of debt instruments compare in terms of the timing and amount of their cash flows. The vertical access shows the monthly amount of the payment, if paid, and the horizontal axis shows the month (1-60). The chart excludes amounts at the purchase and maturity (redemption).

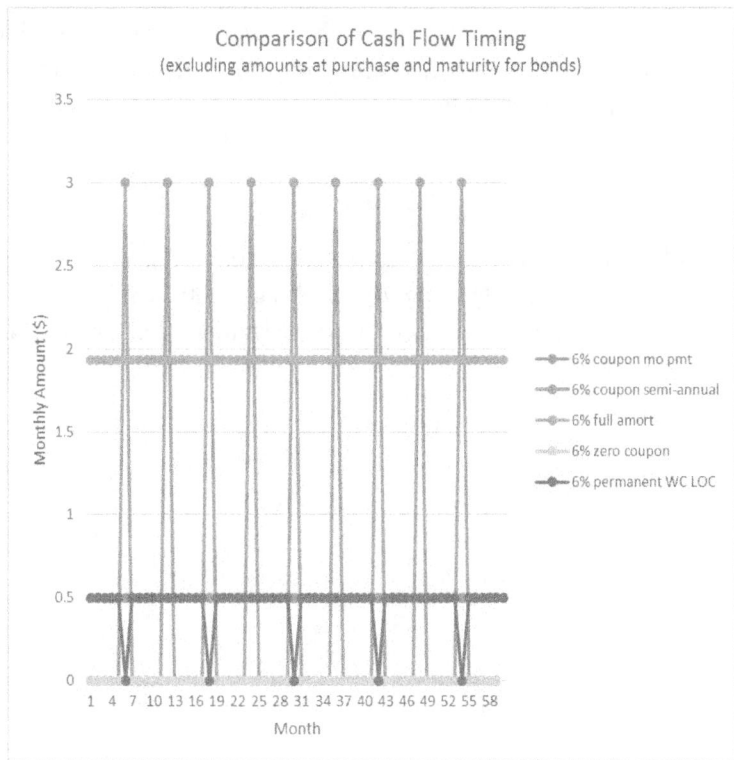

1. The zero coupon bond pays no cash until maturity, so the monthly amount is zero for the period shown (months 1 through 60).
2. The permanent non-amortizing working capital line of credit (labelled permanent WC LOC) that does not pay off at the end of 5 years pays interest of $0.50 monthly except for the months when the credit line is "cleaned up" and left at a zero balance for 30 days to remain in accordance with the terms of the credit line agreement.
3. The plain vanilla bond has zero cash flow until the semi-annual payment of $3 is made.
4. The fully-amortizing term loan has a steady monthly cash flow of $1.93 which includes both principal and interest in the monthly payment, and pays off in full in the final month.
5. The line of credit that pays off at maturity (the debt labelled 6% coupon monthly payment) provides a steady monthly cash flow of $0.50.
6.

Comparison of Total Cash Flows

The following chart compares the sum total of cash flows for each debt instrument. *Net of principal* in the chart subtitle refers to debt that was redeemed at maturity; if not redeemed, the principal is not deducted.

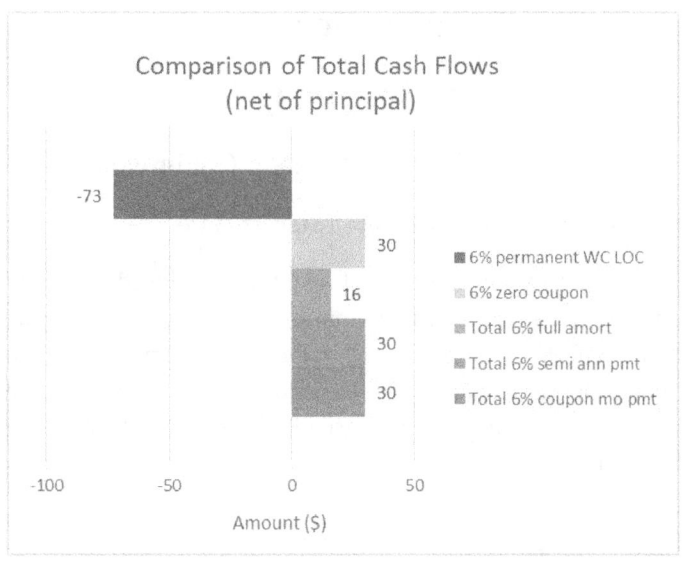

Comparison of Total Cash Flows
(net of principal)

-73

30

16

30

30

- 6% permanent WC LOC
- 6% zero coupon
- Total 6% full amort
- Total 6% semi ann pmt
- Total 6% coupon mo pmt

-100   -50   0   50

Amount ($)

1. The zero coupon bond pays a total of $30 of interest.
2. The permanent non-amortizing working capital line of credit (labelled permanent WC LOC) pays a negative $73 because the principal balance is *not* redeemed at maturity. *(Note that the credit line was "cleaned up" and left at a zero balance for 30 days once each year to remain in accordance with the terms of the credit line agreement).*
3. The plain vanilla bond pays $30.
4. The fully-amortizing term loan pays $16 of interest and returns the principal progressively during the loan term.
5. The line of credit that pays off at maturity pays a total of $30 (the debt labelled 6% coupon monthly payment)

APPENDICES

APPENDIX 1

Economic Growth and Interest Rates: Commentary

The Macroeconomic Equilibrium Interest Rate

The following shows an example of a simplified closed economy simultaneous equation macroeconomic model from which the equilibrium interest rate equation in Part II is derived. In that equation, autonomous taxes, government expenditures and the money supply are independent variables that impact upon the equilibrium interest rate.

$$y_t = c_t + j_t + g_t$$

$$c_t = \alpha + \beta yd_t + e_t \qquad\qquad (\alpha > 0, 0 < \beta < 1)$$

$$j_t = \zeta + \theta r_t + e_t \qquad\qquad (\zeta > 0, \theta < 0)$$

$$yd_t = y_t - t_t$$

$$t_t = \tau + \varepsilon y_t + e_t \qquad\qquad (\tau > 0, 0 \le \varepsilon < 1)$$

$$ms_t = md_t$$

$$md_t = \lambda + \phi y_t + \varphi r_t + e_t \qquad\qquad (\lambda, \phi > 0, \varphi \le 0)$$

The demand side of national income. The above identity $c_t + j_t + g_t$ represented a *demand-side approach* to national income accounting and the variable y_t is called *aggregate demand*.

Aggregate demand is equal to and alternatively referred to as *gross domestic product* (GDP). For an *open* economy model, the *aggregate demand* identity adds exports x and imports m as follows:

$$y_t = c_t + g_t + j_t + x_t - m_t$$

The functions of the model are consumption c_t, investment j_t, tax t_t and money demand md_t. yd_t is *disposable income* which is obtained by deducting taxes t_t from income y_t. .

In this type of model, the type of interest rate may not necessarily be clarified; however, in a modern centrally planned context, interest rates may tend to move in tandem beginning with policy interest rates, with equilibrium eventually being reached in bond yields; bank loan rates may move in a similar direction through the banking system.   In any event, the net effect is a rise in borrowing costs which raises the concerns expressed in the fiscal policy effectiveness and crowding out debate, discussed below.

This demand-side approach to representing national income has traditionally been popular as an analytical tool in part because it is assumed that increased spending, in particular government spending g can help boost economic growth. This approach also may serve to obscure the foundational role of businesses/firms in the accounting.

Defining Economic Growth

There are a number of critical problems with treating increased expenditures and demand as growth, and in particular, government expenditures as a source of economic growth. One major problem concerns the definition of "growth" itself. Another relates to equating demand with supply.

Several matters are addressed below, beginning with the poorly understood Say's Law. Special attention should be given to the note on pricing, as well.

1. Supply, Demand and Say's Law

The tendency to equate supply with demand and therefore to ignore the supply side and production in favor of demand-side economics was a pervasive feature of 20th century economics. This confusion may have its origins in an erroneous exposition of Say's Law as traced by William Hutt (1974) to Keynes' *General Theory* (1936: 18). Economists have become accustomed to using the phrase *"supply creates its own demand"* when referring to Say's fundamental economic law.

Hutt attempts to explain the error: "...the supply of plums does not create the demand for plums"...but rather, "...the supply of plums constitutes demand for whatever the supplier is destined to acquire in exchange for the plums...." (1974: 3).

Say's own words may be clearer: "One can only buy with what one has produced," and "the one product constitutes the means of purchasing another" [Say (1803) as cited by Hutt (1974: 25)].

Hutt also provides statements from James Mill (1808) that not only clarifies the meaning, but also suggests that the principle is the source of national wealth through *production and productive activity*: "The collective means of payment of the whole nation...consist in its annual produce" and "(A) nation's power of purchasing is exactly measured by its annual produce." [Mill (1808) as cited by Hutt (1974)].

Policy Prescription. It should be noted that an emphasis on production and the supply side is not an argument in favor of *mercantilism*. Mercantilist policies, in which official policy may protect industry and export production to the detriment of foreign trade, are widespread to this day, in part aided by the coordinated interventions and policies of monetary authorities world-wide.

Pricing: Offer vs. Price. Say's Law also addresses a crucial point regarding "lack of demand" or *demand failures* which provided the justification for stimulus policy and boosting demand through debt accumulation and low interest rates.

However, Say's Law helps explain that the apparent lack of demand is the result of something else: Defects in the *pricing process* (Hutt, 1974: 8). First, some background as the topic of prices appears simple but can be confusing: Price *offered* is not the same thing as a price. An item offered at a price twice what people are willing to pay is not a price, only an *offer* to sell at that price. Prices reflect items actually bought and sold. The decision to buy and sell (at a price) is based on the costs and benefits perceived by buyers and sellers (given available information). If the offered price is not eventually reduced due to lack of "takers" (buyers at that price), the item is said to be *withheld* from the market.

Items withheld from sale because prices offered are too high from the perspective of potential buyers *appears* to cause a demand failure because people aren't buying at that price. Therefore, the traditional Keynesian solution is to supply the economy with more debt through lower interest rates and other policies, which only adds to the problem of over-indebtedness and financial distress.

Under normal competitive market conditions businesses would sooner or later be expected to price their products to sell. An interesting question is then how some businesses are able to temporize (wait) for extended periods of time and not offer their products so that they sell (i.e. offer their products at "market-clearing prices). A simple answer is that for whatever reason, the cost to the business for waiting is low. If these costs are low enough, an economic investigation may reveal that there are likely (non-market) various policy and regulatory factors propping up businesses--including those originating from the financial system and interest rate policy-- *that allow financial losses or loan non-repayment of these businesses to continue indefinitely.* The problem of permanent non-amortizing working capital credit lines is highlighted in the discussion on the banking system.

2. Crowding Out and Fiscal Policy Effectiveness

Interest rates are also central to the topic of fiscal policy effectiveness and *crowding out*. Fiscal policy may be defined as the use of government spending and tax policy to spur economic growth, with growth being defined normally as GDP growth. Bond-financed government spending in theory crowds out (or displaces) private investment by causing a rise in interest rates that suppresses borrowing and ultimately is assumed to cause government spending to be an ineffective policy tool. Conclusions as to the effectiveness of fiscal policy in part depend on assumptions with regards to the true nature of interest-rate elasticities of money demand and investment in the traditional Hicksian IS-LM framework. For an empirical study on this debate for an Asian economy during the late 20th century, see Kennedy (1999).

Although the crowding out debate may appear to have some basis in Keynesian economics, from the famous *The General Theory of Employment, Interest and Money* by John Maynard Keynes (1936), Carlson and Spencer (1975) trace the beginning of the crowding out controversy to empirical work and supporting studies from 1968 to 1970 (1975:3). *General Theory* may have provided some argument in favor of the effectiveness of government spending, but interestingly, Carlson and Spencer (1975: 5) add that "(I)t is ironic that certain passages …provide strong support for the opposite contention."

Some important conclusions may be drawn from the above discussion on fiscal policy effectiveness and crowding out:

A. Interest rate suppression. Assuming that in theory interest rates could rise due to government bond issuance, the crowding out thesis may have in practice been virtually irrelevant. Why? Because central banks can generally be expected to provide sufficient liquidity and enter as a buyer into the bond market to suppress unwelcome rises in interest rates/yields. In a low or near-zero nominal interest rate environment, central banks may even emerge as dominant buyers of government bonds where investors may have retreated due to poor anticipated returns.

B. Debt Bias: Debt as a substitute for income. Although firm conclusions regarding the effectiveness of fiscal policy may remain elusive, the dominant concern in this controversy has always remained the prevention of rising interest rates. Such a focus suggests an inherent bias in favor of debt accumulation as a substitute for income in order to produce economic stimulus: Essentially meaning encouraging more borrowing to invest and spend. This logic appears to be the opposite of earlier economic theory, in which profitability was a pre-requisite for payment of interest (Smith, 1976). Considering the controversy's beginnings (1968-1970), the groundwork may have been established for the inflationary 1970's in the U.S. that followed.

The term *financialization* of an economy and similar references might also be used to describe the use of debt growth through the financial system as a replacement for real income growth, beginning in the latter part of the 20th century. (Stockman, 2013)

3. The Government Budget Restraint (GBR)

A perhaps more compelling argument than crowding out is the government budget restraint (GBR), also referred to as the government budget constraint (GBC). It is easily assumed that government expenditures originate from an external source that injects stimulus into the economy and possibly invoking the image of a "manna from heaven." However, the seminal work of Carl Christ (1968, 1979) accounts for the *sources of government financing*: Taxes, bonds and high-powered money (also called *base money*). Taxes originate involve the removal of money from one part of the economy to put elsewhere according to various political priorities. Government bonds are issued to borrow from the public or other entities, including financial institutions and central banks. The central bank can produce high-powered money by purchasing assets, most notably government bonds when government expenditures exceed tax revenues (resulting in deficits).

The international dimension to the sources of financing could be added. This includes high-powered money financing by *foreign* central banks, which (in the case of the U.S., for example), can purchase U.S. government bonds (Treasuries) as part of their currency policies, providing a source of financing to the U.S. government that does not necessitate the creation of high-powered money by the monetary authority of the U.S (i.e. the Federal Reserve); the high-powered money creation rests with the foreign countries in their currencies.

Each of these sources of government financing as can be thought to have consequences and costs to the economy, including disincentives to produce (due to real or perceived excessive taxation), over-indebtedness due to artificially lowered interest rates, inflation due to money creation (causing potential hardship for individuals on fixed incomes, even at moderately low but sustained inflation), or debt-based deflation during a *credit crunch* when over-indebtedness causes systemic banking problems and lending contraction.

The net effect over long periods of time of these consequences can be greater debt accumulation and lower income to service the debt—the opposite of policy objectives and what might be considered desirable for economic expansion.

4. Investments (Outflow) and Returns (Inflow)

A focus on profit alone is insufficient for the analysis of investment and growth. A *return* on an investment is not known unless there is an investment associated with a profit. Clarification can be found in the field of corporate finance:

Discounted cash flow (DCF) analysis. In corporate finance the net present value of an investment is calculated by discounting future cash flow by an appropriate interest/discount rate (also called the opportunity cost of capital). However, the investment is a single cash *outflow* while the amounts to be discounted are expected future cash *inflows*. (Brealey and Meyers 1996): That is, the directional flow is *opposite*.

In national income accounting, investment is treated as an expenditure like other expenditures, and directionally the same. However, investing is fundamentally different from consumption. Investments are generally made in order to generate or receive an income (out of profit) and therefore a *return* on the investments. This applies to both firms and individuals alike. For firms, there are a number of measures of return on investment such as ROI and returns that can be calculated with DCF and other types of analysis. For investors, returns on equity and debt investments are derived from profitability (defined here as *NCF-D* in the discussion on primary SOR); the dividends/distributions and the debt service (principal + interest) are the returns (inflows) on those investments (outflow) that once again, are *opposite directional flows*.

Policy interest rates and capital appreciation. It is critical to note that the particular *return* being referred to here should not necessarily include *capital appreciation* which as stated earlier can be influenced by an external source (such as policy interest rates) that is not linked to the economic entity's own financial performance. Capital appreciation of equities can occur frequently that is unrelated to official interest rate policy, but rather, based on the profitability and improved outlook of the firm itself.

The following diagrams are intended to clarify a relationship that describes growth as a *return on investments* and which may ultimately be a foundation for self-sustaining economic expansion.

Diagram 1. Returns on investment as economic growth. The first diagram describes the framework of an economic entity such as a business including self-employment, and organizations such as non-profits. NCF is Net Cash Flow as discussed elsewhere, and a positive figure is considered a pre-requisite for self-sustaining

69

(sustainable) growth; negative NCF may occur. For companies/entities that pay dividends/distributions, these are deducted from NCF and provide a return to the owners/equity holders. For entities that do not pay dividends/distributions, any positive NCF would be expected to be reinvested in the operations of the business. Next, debt service (principal + interest) can be paid to debtholders (e.g. investors in bond, creditors), providing them with a return on their debt investments. As for organizations that do not have in their mission to make a profit (i.e. non-profits), if they have taken on debt they would generally need to have a sufficient "fund surplus" that can be used for debt service.

Diagram 2. Savings and investment flow. In the second diagram, the logic of returns on investment can still apply to individuals and households. While dividends/distributions in a business sense do not exist; amounts taken out of savings can be investments of various kinds and not all which may have a clearly tangible return. For certain types of investments a return in monetary terms may not always be identifiable and can involve key benefits as support, care, friendship or possible groundwork for future business relationships or as-yet unknown sources of income.

The two diagrams are shown below:

RETURNS ON INVESTMENT AS ECONOMIC GROWTH

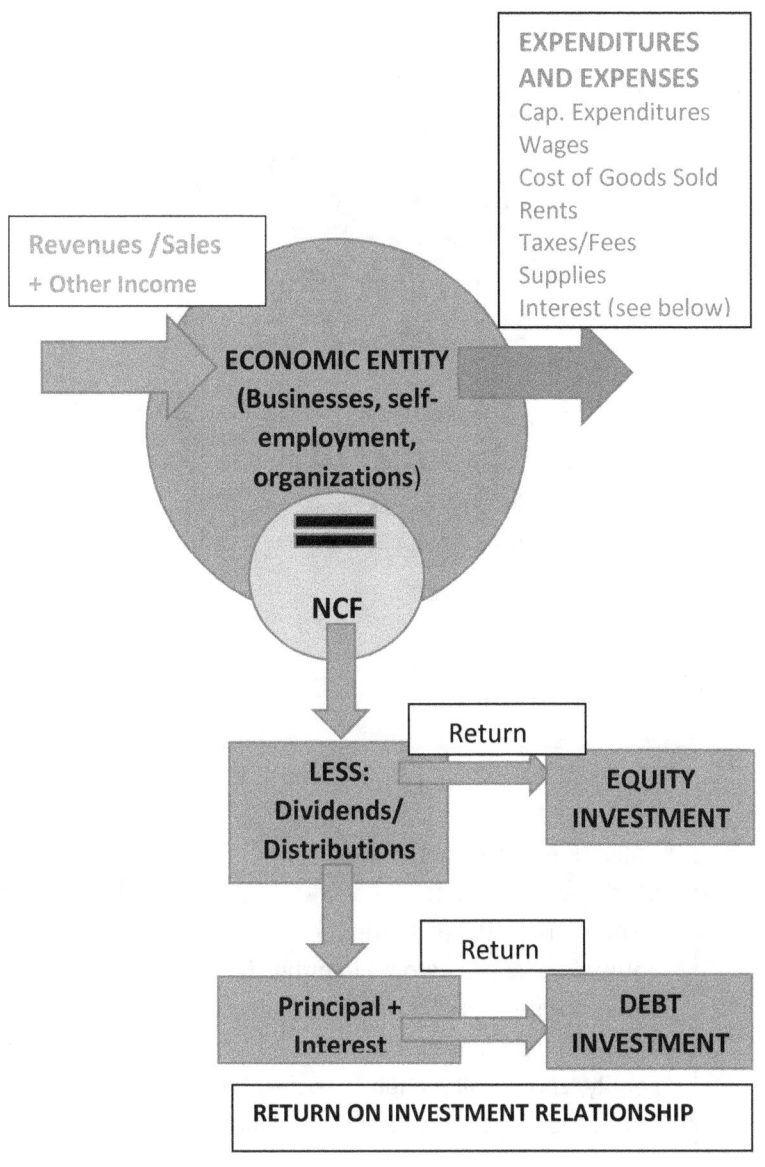

SAVINGS AND INVESTMENT FLOW

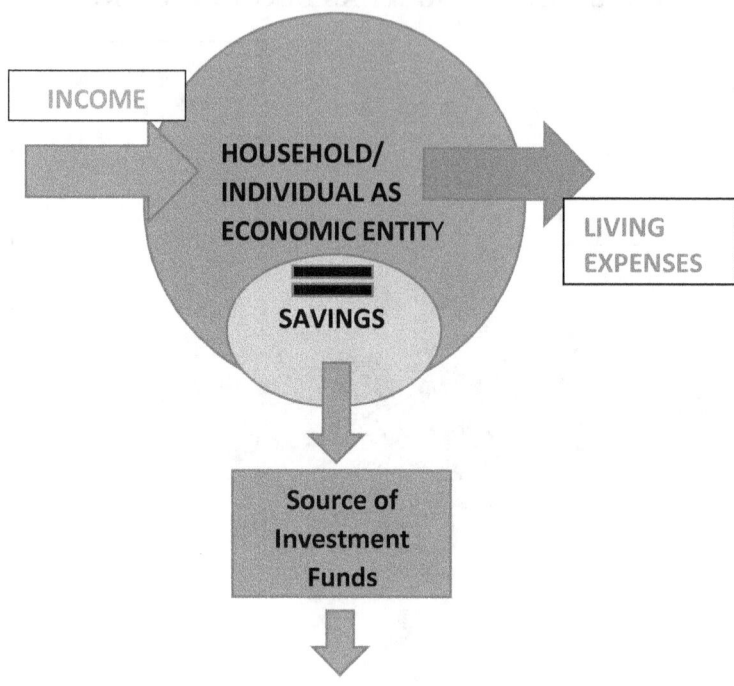

INCOME

HOUSEHOLD/
INDIVIDUAL AS
ECONOMIC ENTITY

SAVINGS

LIVING
EXPENSES

Source of
Investment
Funds

INVESTMENT EXAMPLES (returns not shown)
*Cash and equivalents, currencies
*Collections, precious metals, etc.
*Land and Real Estate
*Debt instruments (e.g. bonds)
*Equity (e.g. shares/stocks in public firms)
*Other equity (other businesses, self-
employment business, etc.)
*Family, community, church, social capital
*Marketable skills development, calling

Real Economic Growth: Expenditures vs. Investment Returns.

A rethinking of the traditional approach of referring to "economic growth" simply as growth in spending and GDP is suggested. A full accounting of the financing sources for government spending (Christ 1968, 1979) coupled with a better understanding of balance sheet accounting (as in the *Assets=Liabilities + Equity* of ordinary financial accounting) are critical to identifying the *accumulation of debts* associated with spending growth as well as the *growth in the money stock that also provides a source of financing*; the latter is covered below.

An alternative approach to defining "economic growth" would be growth of real *investment returns* (adjusted for *currency dilution* to arrive at a more comprehensive *real* measure of returns expressed in national currency units), rather than expenditure growth (adjusted for common measures of inflation). *Currency dilution* is discussed further below. Real investment returns in this sense incorporates ordinary accounting measures and also may ultimately lay the groundwork for fundamentally lasting economic expansion.

Money Creation, Debt and Inflation. With regard to money creation and inflation, it is acknowledged that base money can still be produced in large quantities without a concomitant rise in inflation. Also, price inflation may occur at times and at rates that do not necessarily correspond to the timing and growth of the money creation. The process of fractional reserve credit expansion through the lending out of excess reserves is expected to be a far more significant inflationary force but inflation can easily be confused with "growth" since in nominal terms incomes appear to be rising.

Debt saturation. Credit expansion and money creation may at times in an economic cycle be impeded by a number of factors that originate in over-indebtedness engendered by a debt-bias in economic policy. Credit impairment of the banking system (e.g. non-performing loan portfolios), and a weak propensity to borrow by firms and individuals can then result in a slowdown of the process. When a hypothetical "debt saturation" has been reached, firms and households no longer are capable of servicing their debts; borrowers become poor credit risks and are declined for further credit (this does not imply that it would be appropriate to ignore basic credit principles to extend credit indefinitely as the problems of over-indebtedness would be expected worsen by prolonging a debt bias).

Currency dilution and the money stock. National money can be created either through the creation of high-powered money (base money) by the central bank or through lending by the banking system in the process of fractional reserves expansion. This money growth, when financing various expenditures, represents additional currency units that dilute the existing stock of currency. These additional currency units may appear as a form of income and raise apparent profitability, but because they are dilutive, must be deducted to obtain real measure of investment returns.

Common measures of inflation such as CPI and the WPI may not accurately reflect the amount of currency dilution occurring in an economy. Consequently, when attempting to calculate a measure of *real interest rates* (using the Fisherian real interest rate formula) and *real investment returns*, incorporation of information on the stock of money in a balance sheet sense could assist in accounting for currency dilution by subtracting nominal money supply growth for the same period

Accounting for returns on investment. National income accounting is a highly specialized area of accounting; a very basic sketch is provided here. National income can be referred to as *gross domestic product* (GDP) or *aggregate demand* (AD) as noted above, and is an approximate measure of the *value added* to an economy seen from the perspective of both income and expenditures; total income should be equal to total payments. *Income* categories of national income accounting are also familiar in ordinary accounting: Wages, interest, rental income, indirect business taxes (excise taxes), capital consumption allowance

74

(depreciation), corporate profit taxes, debt service and retained earnings (undistributed profits).

Suppose that the *total value of output* of firms is 120 (roughly corresponding to the *total revenues* by firms in an ordinary financial accounting sense). Say that *inter-firm purchases* are 20 (somewhat related *cost of goods sold* in financial accounting). Subtracting these *inter-firm purchases* (20) from the total *value of output* (120) should give us the *value added* to gross domestic product (GDP) of 120-20=**100**. This *value added* figure of 100 corresponds roughly to *gross profit* in an ordinary accounting sense, and should be equal to the sum of the *income categories* as stated above (wages, interest, rental income, etc.).

Closing reflections. Accounting for return on investment requires the directionally opposite relationship between a *profitability measure* (i.e. the cash inflows in the corporate finance sense noted above) and investment (i.e. the initial cash outlay for investment as noted above). As a rough guide, an aggregate version of the *NCF-D* measure (or perhaps *corporate savings*) could be a proxy for profitability, with non-consumption as a possible proxy for investment. Then, to obtain *real* measures, the growth in currency dilution can be deducted for the same period of observation.

APPENDIX 2

Identifying the Primary SOR for Debt Service

1. Primary Source of Repayment (SOR)

The primary source of repayment for servicing a debt is considered to be *Net Cash Flow less Dividends/Distributions*. This appendix begins with an explanation of the process of arriving at *Net Cash Flow* (NCF), then deducts cash dividends/distributions to arrive at a proposed definition of the primary source of repayment. Next, certain refinements to NCF are proposed. The final section covers the topic of *alternative* sources of repayment.

Analysts appear to be divided in the use of accrual-based and cash flow measures as a primary source of repayment. Moreover, the term "cash flow" can be defined in a number of ways, not all of which can reasonably considered to be a primary source of repayment when examined more closely; various approaches to defining cash flow should be sorted through and classified.

To begin, a distinction is drawn between two common terms, *accrual earnings* and *cash flow* (cash flow also can include *accrual earnings-based* cash flow). Clarifications will be provided below.

Accrual Earnings. Accrual-based net earnings cannot be viewed as a source of repayment for debt service. The terms "net profit" "net income" and "net earnings" and "earnings" can be used interchangeably, and are assumed to be accrual-based unless otherwise indicated. The term "cash flow" has numerous possible definitions and is explained below.

Cash Flow

The term "cash flow" can give rise to considerable confusion as well as error. Two types of "cash flow" can be identified: The first type of cash flow measure *is accrual earnings-based* and is considered to be an incomplete source of repayment. The second type centers on the concept of *free cash flow*, and is considered to be a reasonable approximation to a source of repayment for debt service. Each type is described below.

Cash Flow (Accrual Earnings-Based). The following measures of what is often referred to as "cash flow" are considered inadequate because they ignore essential cash (out)flows, in particular *capital expenditures* (abbreviated *capex*) and *changes in working capital*. Their formulas are based on accrual earnings figures, with certain non-cash items added back, as follows: (*Net income + depreciation)* or (*Net income + depreciation +*

amortization). This definition may also sometimes be called *funds flow*. Another measure of cash flow, EBITDA, is earnings before interest, taxes, depreciation and amortization.

It could be argued that depreciation is a reasonable approximation for capex, and therefore can be used in its place. However there is evidence that the amount of depreciation can fall short of the actual capital investments required and therefore cannot necessarily be assumed to be cash flow available to cover debt service. In a sample of 51 firms that had defaulted on their debt, 69% of the companies had invested *more* than their depreciation amounts and the EBITDA measure overestimated cash flow interest coverage prior to default. (Moody's 2000: 4) While EBITDA *less capex* could be used to correct for the overstated cash flow, changes in working capital remain unaccounted for.

Cash Flow--Best Approximation. The following examples are measures of cash flow that are considered to best approximate a primary source of repayment for debt service: NCF and FCF; both of these measures account for capital expenditures and both capital expenditures and changes in working capital.

NCF. Hitchner (2011) uses the term *net cash flow* or *net free cash flow* (both abbreviated as NCF). The formula for NCF is Earnings before interest and taxes – taxes on EBIT at effective tax rate + depreciation – capital expenditures plus/minus changes in working capital. (2011:500) NCF to overall invested capital is associated with both debt and equity and is also called *invested capital net cash flow*. (Hitchner, 2011:648).

FCF. The corporate finance literature also uses *free cash flow* (FCF) in security valuation. Rosenbaum and Pearl (2013) compute free cash flow starting with earnings before interest and after taxes (EBIAT). Their formula for FCF is:

FCF=EBIAT + Depreciation and Amortization - Capex - increase/ (decrease) in net working capital (2013: 131, 163).

Because of their similarity, NCF and FCF may often be used interchangeably.

It is recognized that NCF is not a measure in accordance with Generally Accepted Accounting Principles (GAAP).

In addition to the computations for NCF (or FCF) above, an alternative measure of NCF can be obtained by referring to a company's financial statements as follows: *Net cash from operations* (NCO) from the cash flow statement of a company's financial statements, less capital expenditures (also from the cash flow statement, in the Investing section). NCO may roughly correspond to the formula above for NCF and FCF after adjusting for changes in net working capital but *before* deducting capex.

The preferred term for cash flow as the primary source of repayment for debt service is *net free cash flow* or *net cash flow* (NCF), in accordance with Hitchner (2011). NCF can be defined as the net cash flow from the recurring, essential operations of the business, less capital (and other) expenditures required for the business to remain competitive in its industry.

Further adjustments to NCF are proposed below for the analysis of debt service coverage.

A. NCF less Dividends/Distributions (NCF-D)

In order to arrive at the general definition of primary SOR, NCF is modified to account for *cash dividends* (for public firms that pay dividends) and *distributions* (for private firms and smaller businesses the firm may have *owners' draws* instead of dividends). Draws/distributions are a common form of additional compensation taken in addition to officer's salaries.

Cash Dividends/Distributions. Since NCF is also a source of payment for other non-operating purposes of the business including cash dividend payments/distributions, the primary source of repayment should be NCF *less dividends/distributions* to owners and equity investors (abbreviated as NCF-D).

NCF-D can be viewed as a form of "net profitability" *in a cash flow sense*. Note that when the term "profit" or "profitability" is occasionally used here the meaning of NCF-D is intended unless otherwise indicated.

Priority. The question may arise as to the prioritization of dividends/distributions over debt service (principal plus interest). For a financially sound business performing on its loan agreements, dividends/distributions can generally be assumed to take priority as per the owners/equity-holders with a controlling interest in the business. An exception to this may come into play in a loan "workout" scenario when the business defaults and re-negotiates terms with the lender. Certain contractual arrangements including subordination agreements and "creditor-in-possession" may give the lending institution preferential rights with regards to securing repayment.

Cash dividend payments to be included in the debt service coverage ratio should be recurring cash dividends on both ordinary and preferred shares. Other types of recurring cash distributions should be included. *Special dividends* and *liquidating dividends* could possibly be excluded from computations for *recurring* dividend payments, but should be at least noted as such. Stock dividends would also be excluded.

B. Further Refining NCF

Acquisitions and Other Key investments. As discussed above, capital expenditures are deducted to arrive at net free cash flow (NCF). However, there may be other types of investment expenditures necessary to achieve or maintain dominance in an industry. For example, if a firm tends to make recurring business acquisitions, it could be argued that in addition to capital expenditures, cash outflows for business acquisitions should also be deducted to arrive at a more accurate figure for NCF.

The acquisition of other key investments including businesses may even be viewed as an extension or variation of capex, as both assets and technology transfer are likely integral to the acquisition. Such acquisitions and investments can take many forms, and the terminology may also vary. This could include the following examples which in some cases may represent significant amounts:
Acquisition of licenses, technology and patents
Capitalization of software costs (not included in capex)
Purchases of certain intangible assets
Acquisition of investments in consolidated undertakings
Purchases of long-term investments
Investments in non-marketable equity investments
Acquisition of interests/investments in JVs
Acquisition of investments in associates

Other Uses of NCF. Other uses of NCF include share repurchases, the build-up of cash reserves or investments in various short-term financial instruments for non-operating purposes. Although these uses may be somewhat more discretionary, they may also be deducted from NCF if they are deemed to be a priority for the business.

Accounting for Non-Cash Transactions. Non-cash income potentially overstates cash flow if not properly identified. And special care should be taken to improve the accuracy of cash flow measures. A few examples of non-cash items that can appear to inflate cash flow include: Income/undistributed earnings according to the *equity method* of accounting for investments, gains on inventory due to increased valuation, deferred and amortized gain on sale of assets in sale-leaseback accounting, unrealized gains on marketable equity securities, and minority interest income. Other possibly less-common non-cash transactions include income from litigation or settlements where a receivable is generated but is non-cash until collection. Long-term debt that is converted into a *demand note,* if reclassified into short-term operating debt could inflate operating cash flow.

Financial statements that include a statement of cash flows may adjust for non-cash items. This discussion of non-cash transactions is not comprehensive and each firm and industry may present special cases.

2. Alternative Sources of Repayment

The above section dealt with the primary source of repayment. However, alternative sources of repayment exist and should be identified when evaluating the sources of repayment.

If the primary source of repayment is insufficient to cover debt service, secondary (or tertiary) sources of repayment can be drawn upon to cover the shortfall; this could include liquidation of short-term investments, non-essential assets or the issuance of equity. In a low-interest rate environment, cheap borrowings to (re)finance debt service may be appealing. However, these alternatives may not be without consequences for the firm, and they do not replace *NCF-D* as the primary source of repayment to service the debt of the borrower.

Adam Smith makes an interesting reference to the use of an alternative source of payment in the form of borrowing to service existing debt:

"The interest of money is always a derivative revenue, which if it is not paid from the profit which is made by the use of the money, must be paid from some other source of revenue, unless perhaps the borrower is a spendthrift, who contracts a second debt in order to pay the interest of the first."(Book I, 59)

Exceptions. It should be noted that for certain types of loans, an alternative source of repayment other than the primary SOR may actually be intended as part of the loan arrangement:

Bridge loans do not necessarily amortize and are repaid if there is a non-current asset to sell to pay off the loan, a take-out lender to pay off the loan, or if owners of the business provide an equity infusion to pay off the loan.

In construction financing the initial construction period may involve a non-amortizing interest-only draw line, and when the construction is complete, the loan is rolled into a fully amortizing term loan which may be granted by the same lender or another so-called "take-out" lender.

APPENDIX 3:

Credit Analysis: Other Considerations

As a reference, this appendix lists a number of additional considerations for credit analysis and evaluation.

1. Debt Service and Non-Amortizing Debt

A complexity of the analysis of debt service capacity involves the existence of "problem loans" even if a borrower is capable of servicing the debt with sufficient debt service coverage. This may occur because the loan either does not amortize, or amortizes over such an extended period of time that payments can be made. Such an arrangement can be intentional and part of a restructuring so that the borrower can service the debt more comfortably.

In order to improve the analysis of debt service capacity, the debt service can be divided into amortizing and non-amortizing debt. (Negative amortization is not discussed here). The focus of the discussion will be on non-amortizing debt.

Debt service refers to the return of the principal lent and interest $(P + i)$ through *amortization* of the loan, either full or partial. A schedule of the periodic payments (and the principal and interest amounts contained within those repayments) can be referred to as an *amortization schedule*. Periodic payments can be monthly, quarterly or annual. For example, the debt service payments for a mortgage are typically made at regular monthly intervals. For a mortgage, the loan is scheduled to be paid off at the end of 30 years (or 360 months).

Full amortization. A fully-amortizing loan has a remaining principal balance of zero after the last payment at the end of the term (i.e. the loan is "paid off").

Partial amortization and balloon loans. Loans with an amortization period longer that the term/maturity of the loan are only partially amortized and leave a balance remaining at the end of the loan term (i.e. a balloon); this remaining balance of the loan must be refinanced somehow. An example of such a partially amortizing loan is one with an amortization of 25 years while the loan matures in 5 years.

Non-Amortizing Loans.

These loans are generally interest-only and the principal balance remains over time, with possible pay-downs at the borrower's discretion. These types of loans are discussed below.

Seasonal Credit. A credit line can include "seasonal" credit lines to certain borrowers such as agricultural concerns that have an extended period of time before costs can be recouped at the end of the growing season, for example. A carryover balance, if remaining, may be difficult to roll into a fully-amortizing term loan if the borrower must wait until the next season to produce the cash flow to pay off the loan. This type of loan can carry considerable risk, and the lender must be very familiar with the borrower and the market conditions that will generate the cash flow to repay the seasonal loan.

Credit lines

Business lines of credit typically do not amortize and are interest-only on the outstanding balance. Such standard credit lines are expected to be at a zero balance for at least 30 days throughout the year, referred to as a "clean up" period. The credit line is subject to renewal each year, based on acceptable credit criteria and loan performance.

Purpose. The stated purpose of such lines of credit is for "working capital" which may lead some credit lines to be called *working capital lines* or *facilities*. In theory, a credit line is for very short-term financing purposes. The financing needs can arise from occasional cash shortages due to abnormal and/or temporary cash outflows that exceed the typical period of trading activities. Clean-up of the credit line should be very quick and line should be at a zero balance most of the time).

A reasonable exception to this short-term rule is a fast-growing firm that cannot collect its receivables fast enough to pay its vendors and requires interim financing until growth slows. Once sales level off the receivables collections presumably will provide sufficient cash to pay off the outstanding balance of the credit line. If after the leveling off any carryover debt remains, there would be a need to roll the remaining balance into a fully-amortizing term loan.

Permanent non-amortizing debt. Of particular concern is a tendency for some standard credit lines for "working capital" to become *permanent*, which means a long-term, interest-only, non-amortizing loan. Such loans may appear to be performing well from the standpoint of debt service coverage, as there are only interest payments due each month; as long as the borrower can find a way to "clean up" the line once a year for 30 days, such loans can continue indefinitely. Nevertheless, the principal is likely not able to be returned to the lender, and refinancing with a fully-amortizing loan is likely to cause a problem for debt service coverage.

Certain specialized financial entities do lend against such permanent non-amortizing debt. These include asset-based lending, secured lending, evergreen credit, working capital loans and A/R & inventory financing. These loans they may bear a higher interest rate and are closely monitored by making advances of credit only on evidence of adequate collateral. Contractor receivables are generally not an acceptable form of collateral for such lenders but may be accepted in certain cases.

Banking system. A significant number of these permanent non-amortizing lines of credit may remain in the portfolios of banks that are essentially non-performing loans not being recognized as such. This unamortized (unreturned) capital (principal) may represent a significant drain not only on the return to banks but also a drag on economic vitality. To get a sense of the loss to the banking system, see Part IV for the estimated rate of return on such permanent non-amortizing lines of credit ("dead' capital).

From the standpoint of borrowers, lax lending may initially appear to be appealing, but over the long-term chronic over-lending (by the lender) and over-indebtedness (of the borrower) can engender lax financial and business management practices of the borrower and distort incentives. Beyond a certain point, a bank attempting to recover its principal and increase its return by raising interest rates and/or by refinancing the excessive debt of a borrower may lead to outright bankruptcy of the firm because the borrower may no longer have an adequate primary source of repayment to service the debt.

In severe enough cases where banks are ridden with portfolios of such non-performing, permanent non-amortizing loans and over-indebted customers, bankruptcy of the banks themselves and eventual takeover by the Federal Deposit Insurance Corporation (U.S.) may be a real likelihood.

2. Industry and Capital Investment

A comprehensive credit analysis includes a thorough understanding of the industry in which the firm operates as well as the application of traditional tools of financial analysis.

Although often overlooked, a more in-depth understanding of the composition of the capital expenditures would be highly useful in evaluating firms, and especially for those that tend to be capital-intensive. Capex may often be treated as uniform with little if any distinction made between *maintenance capex* (roughly defined as a level of capex required for the business to maintain its position in the industry), and more technologically advanced capital expenditures intended to propel the firm towards a dominant position in the industry.

3. Quality of Financial Information.

The quality of the source financial information is crucial and can impact upon the results of an analysis of debt service capacity. Even audited financial statements which are considered of high quality may include estimates which may or may not fully and accurately reflect the financial condition of the firm at all times.

Consolidated financial statements remove related company transactions, correcting the sales, cost and liability data and are a critical element in establishing the quality of financial information. *Combined* financial statements are not a substitute for consolidated financial statements.

Small business. For smaller firms with unaudited financial statements, reliability of the financial information is a potentially major issue. A reviewed financial statement may be the best quality available if made available. It is not unusual for smaller businesses to have their financial statements prepared according to a method of accounting other than Generally Accepted Accounting Principles (GAAP), or with significant elements lacking GAAP. This includes cash basis statements and tax returns which are not acceptable substitutes for GAAP-based financial statements. A financial analysis on the basis of non-GAAP information may lead to erroneous conclusions about the company's financial condition.

Complexity and lack of transparency can present a major problem when analyzing smaller businesses without consolidated financial information and quality financial information. Major concerns arise from existence of significant outside entities related by the business owner(s) that are not applying for credit and therefore are not evaluated but whose financial condition can adversely affect the borrowing entity.

For example, in the absence of consolidation, if the principals/owners of a business own commercial real estate (through an LLC or other entity) from which their business leases space, debt service on that real estate should be identified and included in some form of *global cash flow analysis* of the business borrower and related entities [in this case the commercial real estate-owning LLC, and perhaps other entities related by the owner(s)].

Examples of financial quality problems include balance sheets that do not balance (i.e. total assets do not equal liabilities plus equity), missing financial information such as balance sheets or income statements, or relevant schedules. For smaller businesses, cash flow statements may not be available, and typically the credit-granting institution will prepare its own cash flow statements based on the balance sheet and income statement); particular attention should also be paid to financial statements with "unexplained" or "questionable" items including unexplained adjustments to retained earnings, particularly increases).

Occasional misclassification of long-term non-operating assets into operating cash flow can distort the figure upward for operating cash flow in individual years when those assets are liquidated.

For both large public companies and small businesses alike, a change or frequent changes of auditors, CPAs, or tax preparers could be a cause for concern, as well as changes in accounting methods -- proper comparisons with prior periods may no longer be possible.

In the financial statements, *interest expense* may also be classified with "financing costs" or "finance charges" although reporting methods may vary. From the perspective of the analyst, financial statements (including those of high quality) can sometimes present interest figures and debt service data in such a way that a time-consuming search through the *Notes to the Consolidated Financial Statements* may be required.

4. Sufficient Financial History

The quality of financial information is a prerequisite for credit analysis, but without an adequate historical data on the firm, identification of deteriorating fundamentals may be impossible. The business should have a substantial track record in its industry and consistency of financial performance can be identified with more historical data. Reliance on a good year or two of sales and profitability is not sufficient to be regarded as a basis for lending. Moreover, so-called accounting trickery can occur and may be difficult to detect over short periods, particular with a single year of data. However, over longer periods of time, a truer picture of the company's financial condition may emerge.

A minimum of three to five years of financial history is desirable. If data are obtainable, as many as seven to ten years is preferable; although this may be impossible to obtain from smaller firms.

Additional historical data can not only help identify the development of a long-term trend, but aids in comparisons between long-term trends and recent performance. For capital expenditures, an overall pattern may not be identifiable over the short-term and can in some industries can vary significantly from year to year.

5. Independence

Critical to analysis is to identify whether a portion of revenues or expenses involves large *related-party transactions/relationships* that represent a lack of independence and control by the borrowing entity.

Customer concentrations including reliance on revenue from government contracts also should be examined closely.

6. Retention of Owner Capital

While owner distributions/draws are expected, a possible source of credit risk is a pattern of little or a declining amount of capital being retained in the business. This could signify that owners are "cashing out" of the company and might be using debt to substitute their ownership interest. A possible warning sign of problems with the business includes a decline in the principal(s) ownership percentage of the business without explanation.

7. Loan Purpose

A fundamental aspect of the credit decision involves understanding the specific purpose of the loan. However, the purpose may not always be clear, or the stated purpose may differ from the actual intent of the borrower. A potential borrower may be reluctant to state that the loan request is to pay off existing debt (due to being asked out of another bank or financial institution), to cover losses of the firm, to give the owner(s) a big bonus, to buy a luxury car for the owner to use in business (as well as for personal use), or to use funds to funnel cash to an ailing related business entity (that is not the borrowing entity).

The true purpose may be clarified by analysis of the company's financial information (cash flow) to identify where significant outflows of cash may have occurred. Once the purpose can be properly identified, the term and amortization of the loan can be better decided upon.

A serious problem can occur in the granting and subsequent management of credit lines, as discussed above in the topic of debt service and non-amortizing loans. With perhaps some exceptions as noted, the credit line should only assist in short-term financing needs to cover a gap in receivables and payables (or perhaps for occasional unusually large purchases of inventory to take advantage of heavy discounts), and the line would be expected to be clear much of the year. Note that it may not be impossible for a borrower to find two banking institutions that allow one credit line to pay off the other credit line so as to abide by the 30-day "clean-up" period requirement. Depending on the quality and timing of the financial information it may be possible to omit information revealing a relationship with a second (or third) financial institution that permits such payoffs and pay-downs. In such a manner, the credit line can remain a (nearly) permanent, non-amortizing interest-only loan.

8. Financial Ratio and Economic Analysis.

Having settled on *NCF less dividends/distributions* (NCF-D) as a reasonable approximation of the primary source of repayment for debt service, NCF-based financial ratios can be used to further evaluate debt service capacity. The ratios examined are the NCF ratio, NCO/Revenues and Capex/Revenues ratio. A ratio for NCF-D is not examined here because it is assumed that the decision regarding dividend payments and increases may be influenced initially by trends in NCF (although this could be given further attention in future research). The NCO/Revenues and Capex/Revenues ratios are presented in the context of a discussion on economic theory.

Deteriorating Trends and the NCF Ratio. It may not possible to draw a conclusion regarding the desirability of revenue growth without consideration of the net cash flow (NCF) generated out of those revenues.

Each case would need to be examined separately, but a case which could be overlooked is one in which dividend coverage appears to be improving due to rising NCF in *absolute* terms. However, NCF relative to revenues may provide a better basis for evaluation: NCF rising more slowly than revenues may signal a secular weakening in the firm's capacity to support dividend repayments. A simple yet fundamental metric using the primary source of repayment in the numerator and revenues in the denominator can be applied to capture such a relative deterioration: *Net free cash flow/Revenues* (NCF/Revs). This ratio can be referred to as the *NCF Ratio* (or *FCF ratio* if the term *free cash flow* is preferred).

From the example above, if revenues for the year were 400, the NCF ratio would be calculated as 40/ 400 = 0.10

Another case is that of *declining* revenues associated with a rising NCF relative to revenues. While revenue declines may generally be viewed negatively, there may be less cause for concern if the lower revenues are over the long-term still capable of generating increasing net cash flow relative to revenues and the debt service coverage remains adequate or is improving.

Economic Theory. Two main component measures of NCF, net cash from operations (NCO), and capital expenditures (Capex), and their relationship to revenues *NCO/Revs* and *Capex/Revs* may offer additional insight regarding the strength of the primary source of repayment. Does poor performance in these ratios originate from poor management or from the broader economic environment (or a combination of both)? Economic theory may help provide some clarity.

Certain external forces such as monetary policy may be more difficult for individual managers to control and can have both beneficial and negative influences on the firm. A rough sketch is provided here with an example of a policy of lowering interest rates, which can stimulate additional activity that would otherwise not have occurred, and set into motion a variety of events.

Consumers may benefit from lowered interest rates, both in the form of cheaper borrowing costs to finance the purchase of consumer goods, but also in the form of savings on existing debt service obligations such as mortgage repayments (assuming refinancing at a lower interest rate). The savings can increase disposable income and spur purchases that otherwise would not have been made in the absence of the lowered interest rates.

Firms may benefit from the policy (at least temporarily but possibly over longer periods to the degree that the expansion continues), from a boost in their revenues and net cash flow from operations (NCO). It is also possible that the policy may push up consumer goods prices somewhat to induce firms to supply the additional volume of purchases.

In a rising interest-rate environment, the reverse may occur, leading to falling revenues and NCO.

NCO. It is expected that astute managers can find ways to improve NCO by controlling expenses and managing operating assets more efficiently such as through improved receivables or inventory turnover.

However, when the company receives a boost in revenues and NCO from expansionary monetary policy measures, managers may be pleased with the results and not perceive any underlying problem associated with this external factor. Unfortunately, in the opposite case of a contractionary policy environment, layoffs and other cost-control measures may need to be implemented with a severity that would not have otherwise occurred.

Capex and Capital Goods Markets. Capital expenditures may present a different challenge to management. While managers may appear to be acting rationally, the external signal generated by monetary policy may bias decision-making and have long-lasting consequences for firms as described below.

As noted above, if consumer goods purchases are progressively rising over time as the expansion continues, the argument for adding more capital equipment than would have otherwise been purchased may be considered justified. Moreover, the decline in interest rates can stimulate additional borrowings by firms as the purchase of capital equipment appears more profitable.

It should be clarified that change in monetary policy alone is not necessary to spur an industry-wide increase in capital expenditures. A recent technological advance may encourage firms industry-wide to increase capital investments utilizing the technology. However, accommodating policy interest rates could give an extra push towards more investments in such equipment than would have otherwise been the case.

Firms throughout an industry may tend to act similarly, collectively boosting their investments in capital equipment at approximately the same time, and possibly influencing an upward movement of the prices of capital goods.

A major concern is that later in the cycle, firms may suffer serious consequences. The collective overproduction of the goods produced by the overinvested capital equipment may lead to steep price declines of those goods, dissipation of profitability, possible losses and in extreme cases, default and bankruptcy. Firms that rely heavily on capital expenditures may be more adversely affected than those in other less capital-intensive industries, suffering higher capex costs relative to revenues at the outset, and bearing the brunt of greater relative consumer goods price declines towards the end.

Cycle phases. If such policy-induced economic cycles can be said to exist, then it also may be possible to break down the phases of the cycle for an industry, whether expansionary, recessionary or relatively "stable." This also may aid in predicting periods during which industry-wide NCF might be more likely to come under pressure, and not necessarily due to normally-distributed random factors or poor management.

In combination with industry analysis and comparison to peers in the industry it also may be possible to pinpoint firms for poor decision-making *independent* of any economic cycles or phases. In such a case, selection of capital equipment may have been inadequate to respond to competition and the market, with possible negative consequences for the firm's long-term debt service capacity.

While it could be argued that in response to an expansionary policy stimulus managers should attempt to refrain from taking advantage of lowered borrowing costs to acquire capital equipment, it may be difficult in practice. Economic cycles featuring expansionary periods and recessions may be characterized by changes in relative prices of capital and consumer goods. (Huerta de Soto 2012). Also see the discussion below on probability theory.

9. Probability Theory and Normality

When conducting statistical analysis, estimates for the arithmetic mean of various financial measures are generally assumed to follow an approximately normal distribution. The central limit theorem provides a basis for the normality assumption, and roughly stated, relies upon the outcomes being generated additively and by numerous small independent processes.

A major concern is whether the primary source of repayment and other variables tend to be influenced by a dominant external force relative to other impacts, and whether some processes may not be independent. This issue has been touched upon in the context of economic theory above, where systemic monetary and financial events may exert a significant impact on economic activity.

Therefore, some form of normality testing could be a useful supplementary tool of analysis. Further research is recommended on the underlying probability distributions and the economic dynamics. Accordingly, attempting forecasting and constructing forecasting models without consideration of the normality assumption could produce questionable results.

In an informal study of non-financial public companies from fiscal years 1988 to 2001 normality testing was conducted on the ratio of net cash from operations to revenues (NCO/Revenues).The evidence suggested that the population was not normally distributed. The computed chi-square value of 9.97 fell outside of the acceptance region for most levels of significance (alpha) with a probability of less than 2% that the population was normally distributed. These informal normality results should in no way be regarded as valid or conclusive. However, the possibility that certain financial measures may not be normally distributed should be given consideration. Clarifying the underlying probability distributions can be instructive in the analysis of debt service capacity and estimation of loan default probabilities.

APPENDIX 4

The Future of Economic Management

A final point concerns an economy where excessive debt has accumulated, described by a general inability of entities and households to service existing debt. At this point, interest rates may also be approaching the *zero lower bound* to accommodate greater quantities of debt. Further lowering of policy interest rates, declines in real interest rates due to inflationary policies as well as other measures might eventually be effective in encouraging more borrowing and trigger a repeat of another debt-fueled economic cycle and credit expansion through *fractional reserve* banking.

However, there remains the fundamental issue of the historic debt bias and whether debt-based stimulus is an appropriate approach to managing a self-sustaining economic expansion.

Should debt-based growth be deemed an appropriate policy going forward, the question still remains of the possible scenario where monetary authorities find themselves stymied in their attempts to get the debt-based expansion process re-ignited through the banking system. While central banks may aggressively step up purchases of government-issued debt and increasing high-powered money, beyond this level, debt-based growth slows or ceases.

Such a situation might initially be described as recessionary, *deflationary* and depression-like. The issue is perhaps more complex than this, since both deflation and inflation can exist simultaneously in different sectors depending on which are still being propped up by financing and/or regulation; moreover, inflation can be defined in various ways and is not always obvious, a case in point being the shrinkage of package sizes.

It should be noted that although deflation might be publicly blamed for economic problems, it is ultimately the excessive debt brought on by systemic overlending/overborrowing that has made repayment of debt difficult or impossible for many.

While in deflation price declines can bring relief for consumers in the form of price declines, when price declines translate into declining revenues and cash flow for firms, the finances of over-indebted firms and the financial industry alike are threatened. This may eventually pose a seemingly insurmountable problem for monetary authorities.

A rough blueprint is proposed below to manage a transition to a more solid foundation in the 21st century.

From Debt/Spending to Credit/Financial Discipline. A critical step towards solving the problem of over-indebtedness is a transition away from the traditional approach to debt and spending-based political economy.

Monetary authorities can assume a leadership role and guide this transitional process by re-focusing their initial efforts towards the fundamentals of good credit within an economy. This also includes exposure of the financial system to market-based discipline and market-to-market revaluations, which would almost certainly be necessary to ensure self-sustaining compliance and viability. If these protected industries are not progressively exposed to market forces, it is altogether possible that market forces may be naturally imposed upon them in a destabilizing manner. A case in point is the vulnerability of financial institutions to technological advances that can compromise their security due to lagged response times that can occur in highly protected industries.

In addition to ensuring that proper lending practices are being adhered to, combined with exposure to market forces, a comprehensive corrective measures to reduce economic imbalances and poverty would require the following:

1. A rethinking of the foundations of fractional reserve banking which is believed to be destabilizing;

2. Shifting the focus on economy-wide *returns on investment* and wider use of Generally-Accepted Accounting Principles (GAAP).
3. Uniformity of application of the principles of good credit which includes addressing the issue of (a) permanent non-amortizing working capital lines of credit discussed previously; and (b) public entities (governments) which face severe financial problems as is discussed below.

Because of the advanced stage of over-indebtedness that may have developed over a long period of time, managing such a transition would be expected to be exceedingly delicate. Special care would also be necessary to avoid the lure of policy measures to artificially incentivize the economy to "juice' returns, again producing unsustainable distortions and instabilities.

First, it must be recognized that some over-indebted firms may be headed for bankruptcy *regardless* of their level of indebtedness due to their exceedingly poor financial performance. Next, it is important to distinguish between such failing firms and those over-indebted firms that remain viable businesses with a reasonably strong primary source of repayment--*but insufficient to fully amortize the debt on their books*.

Therefore, highly skillful interventions towards economy-wide debt restructuring (which may include partial write-downs and write-offs) could be necessary to avoid mass bankruptcies of *truly viable firms* and in order to restore economic balance. It is acknowledged that many financial institutions may be forced to realize heavy losses on loans in their portfolios that had previously remained unrealized, a painful process that would require highly competent management.

Credit principles for public entities. As stated above, good credit principles should apply uniformly to the extension of credit to both private and public entities. This is particularly urgent given the levels of debt/obligations that many governments have accumulated over the 20th and early 21st century, which includes the unfunded liabilities for pension and health care systems. In some cases public debt levels have reached several times the nation's GDP and have continued to grow: An estimated 23 nations surveyed had debt-to-GDP ratios equal to or exceeding 200% (McKinsey Global Institute, 2015). The IMF (2010) has estimated the U.S. fiscal gap at 14% of the present value of the present discounted value of U.S. GDP (3% discount rate case). Other recent analyses of public debt and fiscal problems are found in Alesina and Giavazzi, Eds. (2013).

As clarified above, a primary source of repayment to service debt is essential to maintaining sound credit principles. A particularly confusing question concerns lending to/financing public entities that traditionally are not seen as generating profits in a financial or economic sense. It is acknowledged that "political profits" may be generated through the political process, and translated into financial benefits for politically-influential special interests--but long-term this appears to have proved disastrous for the finances of government entities, as noted above).

It is evident that *non-profit organizations* can be viable credit risks, although the term "profit" is not used to describe their *surplus* of revenues over expenses. Such entities still are able to manage their operations in such a manner as to produce enough surplus (funds surplus) to be able to service debts they have incurred.

This essential concept can be applied to traditional government entities as well. Part of the restructuring process could entail the redefinition of government entities as (regional) management associations from which their revenues would originate from transparent management fees (replacing traditional taxation) as well as possibly other recurring sources including admission fees, advertising and leasing. Their finances would also need to conform to generally-accepted accounting standards (GAAP) to maintain financial discipline.

In closing, the topic of laying the foundations for economic prosperity is well worth additional consideration in future research.

ADDENDUM

Conventions attempted in the book are mentioned here, although it is recognized that these conventions may not always be consistently applied. **Parentheses.** When a term appears in parentheses after another term [such as *creditors (lenders)*], the meaning of the two terms is taken to be very similar but possibly used in different contexts. The use of "i.e." within parentheses is designed to emphasize the term. "E.g." within parentheses is an abbreviation for "example" as in "for example." Occasionally parentheses will be used in front of or behind another to mean that the word is optional but can help clarify the meaning. **Slashes.** A slash (for example, debt/borrowings) means that both terms are considered to be nearly identical in meaning. **Italics** are added because of its deemed importance and often to indicate a common term in the field that could be researched elsewhere for background information. **Boldface** is intended usually to indicate a subtopic. **Quotation marks** are used either for emphatic effect, for a popularized term, informal jargon or common expression used in a particular field, industry or context. **References.** It can be difficult to cover economic topics without referring to research that might have fallen out of the mainstream, or that is unpopular with certain groups. It was decided that the popularity of a particular view should not necessarily be a basis for inclusion or exclusion of a particular body of thought. **Citations.** A number of citations are sourced from another researcher. It is recognized that a particular citation may not be representative of, or fully convey, the entirety of a body of research and therefore can be misleading if not qualified. Moreover, it is not unusual for some historical writings be confusing or inconsistent. It is understood that some educated guesswork may be necessary at times to ascertain what an author most likely intended to say, as even scholars in the field may be unable to fully agree on the meaning of certain passages.

REFERENCES

Alesina, Alberto and Francesco Giavazzi (Eds.), *Fiscal Policy after the Financial Crisis*, National Bureau of Economic Research (NBER), University of Chicago Press, 2013.

Bohm-Bawerk, E. von., "The Function of Saving" *Annals of the American Academy of Political and Social Science* (May, 1901).

Brealey, Richard A., and Stewart Myers., *Principals of Corporate Finance,* The McGraw-Hill Companies, Inc., 1996.

Brigham, Eugene F., and Houston, Joel F., *Fundamentals of Financial Management*, 10th Edition, South-Western, 2004.

Carlson, Keith and Roger Spencer., "Crowding Out and its Critics," *The Federal Reserve Bank of St. Louis Review*, December 1975, 2-17.

Christ, Carl., "A Simple Macroeconomic Model with a Government Budget Restraint," *Journal of Political Economy* 76 (1) (Jan/Feb 1968), 53-67.

Christ, Carl., "On Fiscal and Monetary Policies and the Government Budget Restraint," *The American Economic Review* 69(3-5) (1979), 526-538.

Damodaran, Aswath., *Investment Valuation: Tools and Techniques for Determining the Value of any Asset*, 3rd Edition

Devajaran, Shantayanan, and Anthony C. Fisher., "Hotelling's Economics of Exhaustible Resources: Fifty Years Later," *Journal of Economic Literature* Vol. XIX (March, 1981), 65-73.

Dornbusch, Rudiger, and Stanley Fischer., *Macroeconomics* (McGraw-Hill 1984).

Fetter, Frank A., "Interest Theories, Old and New," *The American Economic Review*, Volume IV, No. 1 (March 1914), 68-92.

Fisher, Irving., *The Rate of Interest* (New York: Macmillan, 1907)

Fisher, Irving., *The Theory of Interest: As Determined by Impatience to Spend Income and Opportunity to Invest It*, New York, 1930 (1965).

Friedman, David., *Hidden Order* (Harper Business, 1996).

Grant, James., *The Trouble with Prosperity* (Times Books, 1996)

Gray, L.C., "Rent under the Assumption of Exhaustibility," *Quarterly Journal of Economics*, 28 (May, 1914), 466-89.

Hitchner, James R., *Financial Valuation: Applications and Models*, 3rd Edition, John Wiley & Sons, 2011

Hotelling, Harold., "A General Mathematical Theory of Depreciation," *Journal of the American Statistical Association* (September, 1925), 340-353.

Hotelling, Harold., "The Economics of Exhaustible Resources," *The Journal of Political Economy* 39 (2) (April, 1931), 137-175.

Howells, Thomas F., and Edward T. Morgan "Industry Economic Accounts: Initial Statistics for the Second Quarter of 2014", *Survey of Current Business*, Bureau of Economic Analysis, December 2014.

Huerta de Soto, Jesus., *Money, Bank Credit, and Economic Cycles*, Ludwig von Mises Institute 2012.

Hutt, William., *A Rehabilitation of Say's Law*, Ohio University Press: Athens, 1974.

International Monetary Fund, "United States: Selected Issues Paper," *IMF Country Report* No. 10/248, July 2010.

Kennedy, Raoul F., "Econometric Evaluation of Macroeconomic Management: The Case of Fiscal Policy in Taiwan" in *Quantitative Tools in Economic Planning: Applications and Issues in Asia*, United Nations Centre for Regional Development (UNCRD), Research Report Series No. 30, 1999.

Laubach, Thomas and Williams, John C., "Measuring the Natural Rate of Interest," *Review of Economics and Statistics* (Vol 85, No. 4: 1063-1070) November, 2003.

Lundvall, Henrik., and Westermark, Andreas, "What is the Natural Interest Rate?" *Sveriges Riksbank Economic Review* (2011:2).

Keynes, John Maynard., *The General Theory of Employment, Interest and Money*, Macmillan and Co., 1936.

Manrique, Marta., Marques, Jose Manuel., "An Empirical Approximation of the Natural Rate of Interest and Potential Growth" *Documento de Trabajo No. 0416*, Banco de Espana, Madrid, 2004.

McKinsey Global Institute, "Debt and (Not Much) Deleveraging," *MGI Report*, McKinsey & Company, February 2015.

Michaud, Francois Louis., and Christian Upper., "What Drives Interbank Rates? Evidence from the Libor Panel," *BIS Quarterly Review* March 2008.

Mill., James., *Commerce Defended*, 1808.

Miller, Merton H., and Charles W. Upton., "A Test of the Hotelling Valuation Principle," *Journal of Political Economy* 93 (1), 1985.

Moody's Investors Service Global Credit Research, "Putting EBITDA in Perspective," *Special Comment*, June 2000.

Mund, Vernon A., "Interest" (in *Economic Principals and Problems*, Walter E. Spahr (Ed.) Third Edition, Volume II (Farrar & Rinehart, Inc., 1936).

Piketty, Thomas., *Capitalism in the Twenty-First Century*, Harvard University Press, Cambridge, Mass., 2014.

Ropke, Wilhelm., *Crises and Cycles* (adapted and revised by Vera C. Smith), William Hodge and Co,., Ltd., 1936.

Rosenbaum, Joshua., Pearl, Joshua., *Investment Banking: Valuation, Leveraged Buyouts, and Mergers & Acquisitions*, (2nd Ed.), 2013.

Rothbard, Murray N., *America's Great Depression*, Sheed and Ward, Inc., 1975.

Rothbard, Murray N., "Time Preference" in *Capital Theory*, John Eatwell, Murray Milgate and Peter Newman (Eds), W.W. Norton & Company, 1990.

Say, J.B., *Traite d'Economie Politique*, 1803.

Sowell, Thomas., *Say's Law,* Oxford University Press, 1973.

Smith, Adam., *An Inquiry into the Nature and Causes of the Wealth of Nations,* Edwin Cannan (Ed.), University of Chicago Press, 1976.

Stockman, David., *The Great Deformation: The Corruption of Capitalism in America*, PublicAffairs™, 2013.

Wicksell, Knut., *Geldzins und Guterpreise*, (Interest and Prices) Jena, 1898 (English-language translation 1936).

Williams, John C., "The Natural Rate of Interest," *FRBSF Economic Letter* (2003-32), October 31, 2003.

Other Resources

Annual financial statements of the firms in the study were sourced from the filings with the U.S. Securities and Exchange Commission (SEC) or from company annual reports containing financial statements. The NASDAQ, Wikipedia, Wikinvest and Yahoo Finance websites were consulted for financial and other information.